UNLIMITED
OPTIONS

Career Strategies to Last a Lifetime

by

Lily Maestas, MSW
and Lorelei Snyder

PROSPERITY PRESS
Santa Barbara, California

UNLIMITED OPTIONS
Career Strategies to Last a Lifetime
by
Lily Maestas, M.S.W.
and Lorelei Snyder

Library of Congress Catalog Card Number: 96-92047

ISBN: 0-9651077-5-2

Printed in the United States of America

PROSPERITY PRESS
1503 Mountain Avenue
Santa Barbara, CA 93101-4725

Acknowledgments

This book has been a labor of love. As it makes its way into the world, we thank a number of the "midwives" that helped its birthing. To Cork Millner and Michael Larson, who insisted on "passion and humor." To Dr. Howard Figler, Fred Klein, Linda Goodman Pillsbury, Cris Wood, Gary Kravetz, Deb Artz, Michele Jackman, Mary Alice Floyd, Paul Breen, Urban Whitaker, Pamela Trainer, Judy Gumbiner, Betty Christman, and Anne Lowenkoff, who reviewed the material and made cogent suggestions for improvement. To Kathy Lear, our proofreader par excellence. Any mistakes you find were made after she handed it back to us, and therefore, alas, are ours alone. And to Jack Snyder, our computer guru, without whom neither of us would have any hair left.

In addition, Lily has some special thanks.

"I would like to acknowledge and thank the thousands of clients whose perseverance and success have helped me develop The Professional Self Model.

"To Dr. Phillip Gardner from the Collegiate Employment Research Institute at Michigan State University for his encouragement, peer review and recommendations.

"I would also like to acknowledge those people who have actively been involved in my own career development. To my former colleagues at the University of Southern Colorado and San Diego State University who showed me how to work with students and recognize my own strengths. To the staff of the Santa Barbara County District Attorney's Office who demonstrated daily that the value of working for the common good of humanity is the most satisfying work of all and that you can change the world...one person at a time.

"To my current colleagues at Counseling and Career Services, you have been a constant source of inspiration, encouragement and good humor over the years. It is with a great deal of pride and gratitude that I recognize my affiliation with this group of dedicated, creative and highly effective career professionals."

✳ *Dedication* ✳

To Jack and David, who believed and encouraged.

To Samantha and Benjamin, for just being who they are.

Contents

1. Your Professional Self 1
    The Monster of the Unknown 8
    Becoming a Career Consumer 10
    Taking the Show on the Road 10

Why Personal Assessment is So Important 13

2. Inventorying Your Interests 15
    Get Help from the Experts 17
    Visualizing Your Dream Job 21
    Personality/Interest Inventory 25
    Scoring Your Answers 29
    Holland's Occupational Themes 30

3. Identifying Your Skills 33
    Communicating Your Assets 37
    Log on to Your Current Skills 40
    Responsibilities + Skills = Accomplishments 43
    Skill Classifications 46

4. Determining Your Work Values 49
    Discovering What You Want 52
    When You Can't Have Everything 53
    Smell the Coffee 56
    The Company and the World It Operates In 58
    Values Prioritization Exercise 61

5. Identifying Your Personality Style..............67
My World, As I See It.................................*73*
Knowledge is Power..................................*78*
Personal Style Inventory *81*
Personal Style Inventory Scoring Sheet............*85*
Personality Styles in the Workplace...............*87*

Getting Job Market Research to Pay Off.......91

6. Researching Your Options....................93
What in the World is Going On?....................*96*
What's Good in the USA is Good for Me.............*97*
Industry-wise, What's Hot? What's Not?............*99*
What I Can Do For You.............................*102*
Who is Hiring and How Do I Find Them?.............*104*
Straight from the Horses Mouth...................*109*
"Beam Me Up, Scottie!"...........................*112*
First Things First...............................*113*
Resources..*115*

Developing Your Marketing Tools...............125

7. Correspondence that Sells..................127
Cover Letters *127*
Thank You Letters *130*
Clarification Letters *134*
Acceptance/Rejection Or Counter Offer Letters....*136*
Query Letters *140*
Questionnaire *141*
Industry Specific Materials *144*

8. Creating A Convincing Resume...............145
Ambitious Professional Wants Good Title..........*150*

Experienced Administrator Has Done Everything *152*
What Format is Best? *157*
Who You Worked For and How Long *159*
Enhancing Your Image *160*
Beyond Degrees *162*
Putting It All Together *163*

9. Interviewing With Confidence 171
Creating the Sizzle *176*
Selling What You Will Do For The Company *177*
Stacking the Deck in Your Favor *180*
Putting Yourself in Control *184*
My Biggest Fans *190*
The Time, the Place, and Looking the Part *190*
Fifty Questions Frequently Asked at Interviews *193*
Sixteen Attributes Sought by Employers *196*

10. Negotiating 199
Send Up a Trial Balloon *201*
Put Your Terms on the Table *203*
Thank You, But May We Talk Some More? *204*
Identify Your Allies *204*
What Have You Gained? What Have You Lost? *206*
Head 'Em Off at the Pass and Call In the Big Guns *208*
Put It In Writing *211*
Common Negotiable Items *213*

11. Establishing Your Time Line 215
Don't Jump Ship *217*
Help is Out There *218*
The Awful Truth *220*
At This Point in Time *222*
Check Point Charlie *223*

All Work and No Play Makes You Know What 225
Estimated Time Line for Career Changers 227
Estimated Time Line for Active Job Seekers 229

Appendix

The Role of the Career Counselor A-1
Rethinking Your World *A-2*

When and How to Use an Employment Agency B-1

Charts

The Professional Self Model

An Overview...x
A Three Step Process....................................124
Key Words for Success....................................232

About the Authors

Lily Maestas, M.S.W., has developed The Professional Self Model© over her 15 years in career counseling. She has been involved in program development of Career Counseling Centers on university campuses nationwide. Her popular seminars cover issues relevant to the overall career and life planning process. She is widely sought as a speaker and is a columnist and radio personality.

Lorelei Snyder's writing career began over twenty years ago and includes general reporting, editing a community weekly newspaper, and three magazines for which she won several awards. Her freelance articles have appeared in *Toyota Times, Yankee, The Christian Science Monitor, The Business Digest* and *California Bound.*

UNLIMITED OPTIONS
DEVELOPING YOUR PROFESSIONAL SELF
AN OVERVIEW

PART I
ASSESSMENT

◆

IDENTIFIES YOUR
PROFESSIONAL SELF,
WHO YOU ARE, WHAT
YOU CAN DO.

PART II
RESEARCH

◆

EXPLORES
COMPATIBLE
MARKETS WITH
YOUR PROFESSIONAL
SELF.

PART III
MARKETING

◆

DEVELOPS THE TOOLS
TO REFINE, ESTABLISH
AND PRESENT YOUR
PROFESSIONAL SELF.

1 Your Professional Self
Creating a powerful career presence

> *"Your Professional Self is an attitude, created through knowledge, focused through research, and packaged to sell."*

Once upon a time, career change was pursued mainly by unhappy, unfulfilled workers looking for more satisfying opportunities. No longer. In the last few years the employment picture has turned topsy-turvy. "Downsizing" brought with it not just the loss of jobs, but entire career paths. Technology is the driving force that continues to redefine how labor is and will be used, according to Phillip Gardner, Collegiate Employment Research Institute. Manufacturing is moving off-shore. Aerospace engineers are a sacrifice to the peace dividend. Just as the Baby Boomers thought they had arrived, many were ushered out the door. Many more expect to leave their jobs soon, either because they hate them or because they expect to lose them The over 55 crowd is increasingly seen as permanently unemployed. Bureau of Labor Statistics data show that during the 1990-1992 recession, for the first time 55 and older workers lost more jobs than younger workers. Middle managers are a thing of the past. This group accounted for about a third of the corporate jobs eliminated in 1994, but only about eighteen percent of the jobs created, according the American Management Association. No other generation of managers and professionals, whatever their age, has experienced the same degree of job loss and disappointment since the Great Depression.

Career change is in the air, for its own sake, and out of necessity. Even before the downsizing implosion, people changed jobs on average seven times and changed careers three times during their lives.

To be successful moving from one career to the next you must take control of your future. You must develop and become comfortable with what I call your Professional Self, which you create for yourself through attitude, perspective, lifestyle choices, positioning and planning.

We begin our working lives with a somewhat undefined image of who we are and what we want professionally. Oft-times our Professional Self is no more than an aura or ghostlike figure that has some tenuous boundaries but not much substance. Typically it begins with the field we originally chose and trained for in college, with very little thought as to how this would wear in the long term.

✱ *"Why are you here?" I asked the tall, blond, impeccably tailored professional I first met during college career counseling sessions four years earlier.*

"You aren't the only one who wonders," Ellie Fairchild began. "It looked like I had it all, didn't it; like a dream come true. There I was, bright, good-looking, eager. Five major companies clamoring for my favor." She paused a moment. "I made a good choice. The company believe in me, put me on the fast track, and I've doubled my salary since I've been there."

"So what's your problem" I asked.

"I don't like retail, or at least I don't care about it. I'm manager of Accessories now. I have personnel and budgetary responsibility, I can see all the way up the career ladder, and I just can't see myself doing this for the rest of my life. When I think about it, it feels like a nightmare." ✱

> *Your attitude towards your current career and about change is the single most powerful tool you have.*

Your attitude has a tremendous impact on your ability to control the outcome of your life. Viktor E. Frankel, author of the book *Man's Search for Meaning*, and a holocaust survivor, describes this most vividly for me.

After a relatively charmed life as a noted and respected psychiatrist in the Europe of the 20's and 30's, Dr. Frankel found himself stripped to the naked existence of Auschwitz and Dachau. Every circumstance in the concentration camps conspired to make the prisoners lose their hold. All familiar goals in life were snatched away. All that remained was their ability to "choose one's attitude in any given set of circumstances." Those that survived and went on to live productive lives never surrendered their attitude. Attitude became a basic survival skill.

While not as dramatic as Dr. Frankel's situation, losing one's job, becoming disabled and unable to do the work you love, or simply hating what you do, can be as devastating to our personal sense of worth. The concept of attitude often becomes obscured when confronted with a change you don't want to make.

One of the first things we ask someone we meet for the first time is, "What do you do?" A lot of times our self-esteem is based on other people's reactions to our answer to that question, particularly for someone who has been "doing" the same thing for a number of years. The tremendous impact on our ability to interact successfully after losing a job stems from no longer being who we used to be.

Go ahead and mourn the loss of this identity, but along with that, begin to look at what this change can "do" for you. Take a realistic look at what you want from your next employment situation and approach it with the attitude of choice and personal power.

Kathy Sims, director of UCLA's Placement and Career Planning Center, who recently made the transition from a relatively small private university to one of the largest university systems in the country, believes three essential personal qualities are needed to be a successful career changer.

First you must judge your level of hunger. Are you passionate for change? If so, you must channel that passion. Here's where attitude comes in.

What is your quotient for taking risk? You will have to develop strategies to accept the consequences as well as the rewards for that risk.

And finally, you must be able to be yourself and maintain perspective.

"Perspective is the real ticket," she says and I agree with her.

> *You must broaden your perspective; open your eyes and see what choices are out there. What information are you overlooking that could provide unexpected opportunities?*

As you grow in experience, skills and job related talents, your Professional Self will begin to take shape, develop density and become more complex and versatile. The idea of choices emerges as you take control of the path you want your working life to take. The image becomes clearer, sharper, not only to yourself but to the world at large.

> *Your Professional Self is an attitude, created through knowledge, focused through research and packaged to sell.*

This can be one of the most exciting times in your life. You have the opportunity to begin afresh. Now is the time to look at your dreams. What have you always wanted to do? It can also be terrifying.

✳ *I asked Ellie why she didn't change. "What's holding you back?"*
"Do you have any idea how much my dad paid for my college education to get me where I am?"
I nodded.
"What am I supposed to do? Throw that all away? And if I do, what would I throw it away for? How do I know the next thing won't be as disappointing as this?" ✳

A major stumbling block for career changers is fear the next step won't be any better than what they're leaving behind. This concern is legitimate.

"Most people," says Gerald M. Sturman, chairman and CEO of Career Development Team, "find their jobs by hitchhiking. There's very little in the way of real planning. As a result, most of us go through our careers with a vague sense of uneasiness." There are other fears. Fear you have nothing to offer. Fear no one will take you seriously. Fear your first job offer will be your only offer. There is no need to stumble and collapse over these fears. Through these pages you'll develop a road map for identifying, finding and getting the job of your choice. You'll identify and prioritize your work values, giving yourself a framework for evaluating your options. You'll end up with an action plan for success.

✱ Recently, I had a visit from Jim Murchison, a former student, who called to my attention an exercise I once assigned his class regarding the basis of our attitudes about work.

Oh yes! I remembered it vividly because Jim was so upset by what he learned that day.

I asked the class to complete the following statements:

1. My father's attitude about work was...
2. My mother's attitude about work was...
3. My biggest fear about becoming a working adult is...

Through the exercise Jim recalled how much his father hated his job. He had worked for years as a production manager in an industrial firm. He felt stuck in a dead end job, unappreciated by his employer and misunderstood by his colleagues. In short, his work life was lousy, and this feeling spilled over into his family and all other areas of his life. Although the job made him miserable, he kept at it because he felt he had to.

Jim's biggest fear was that what happened to his father would happen to him, and that he, too, would end up in a dead end job, working for somebody he didn't like, doing something he didn't want to do and be there for the rest of his life. As a graduating senior about ready to enter the workforce, it made the future terrifying.

As it turned out, several others in the class shared similar feelings.

"Often times how much you enjoy your work and the degree of control you have over your work environment are directly related," I told them. Jim's father felt no control and believed himself a victim of his workplace.

"This doesn't have to be," I assured them. The better you know who you are and what you have to offer, the more control you have over the choices you make about what kind of work you choose to do, and where you do it. Work can be fun. You can be excited about the time spent at your place of business. You can define your life in positive ways through the kind of work you do and the pleasure you derive from it.

Jim had come back to tell me that after that particular day he had rethought his attitudes and readjusted his ideas of what work was going to be.

"Right after graduation I got a job with a software company that designs video games," he told me. "I'd always been interested in computer games, but was afraid to look for jobs in that field because it didn't seem like 'real' work. You should have heard my dad when I told him. He couldn't believe I was serious."

Jim was now in the research and development division designing computer games and had just been promoted for the fourth time in the last eighteen months. His salary had doubled and he traveled extensively.

"They call me the 'Boy Wonder,'" he chuckled. "I'm having the time of my life, doing what I love in an industry that fascinates me. And you should hear my dad brag about me," he told me as he left. ✳

You'll find this book different in that it stays focused on the job search and career planning process; it organizes the process in a logical sequence, and reinforces each step with consistent application. It's lean and mean, with no fat chapters on "The Job Market," "The Numbers Game," or "The Psychological Trauma of Looking for Work." Each chapter concentrates on a single step, illustrated by a single case study. This method was chosen to show you how my clients have struggled with these problems, worked them through, not without difficulty, and seen their persistence and planning pay off. You can, too.

Each chapter builds on previous work, moving from personal assessment, to research, to marketing yourself. Each subject uses previous skills in conquering the next step, giving the total process a down-to-earth, this-is-how-you-use-this-information emphasis. Through easy-to-use exercises, you'll learn to identify those skills and experiences in your own background that make you a "value adding" candidate to any organization you choose to affiliate with.

This step-by-step process is not for everyone. Each of you enters the career planning process at a different point. Your needs are different at each point. This flexible plan stresses a process that is effective for beginning professionals and applies as well to those in their middle years and beyond. The information you need to make the process meaningful and productive changes throughout your lifetime. The entry level professional contemplating changing jobs for the first time will have needs very different from that of a mid-level manager squeezed out by a corporate merger. Re-entry women and retired military will have different needs. If you need a resume right now, go there directly. If you have an interview scheduled, don't wait for the rest of the book. Once you've addressed your most pressing need, think about the process in total.

> *Most people go through life having their work dictate their lifestyle. I suggest that you shift your priorities to let your lifestyle dictate the work you do.*

Who's responsibility is it to determine what your lifestyle will be? If you want more leisure time, take a long hard look at your finances, figure out how much money you can do without and what that will mean in terms of extras you might have to give up. If you want more prestige or security in your work life, then you may have to seriously deal with the idea of retraining or going back to school to acquire the expertise you'll need to create that lifestyle.

I hear people tell me all the time how they love to travel, but only get two weeks vacation a year. What is wrong with this picture? If you want to travel, find an employer that offers blocks of time off, or better yet, find a position that requires travel. Learn another language, become a tour guide, apply for a job on a Semester at Sea cruise and see the world. I know of one young man who wanted to see the USA at someone else's expense. He went to school and learned to drive 16-wheel tractor-trailers. And he always kept his fishing rod behind the seat.

When was the last time you actually thought about your "dream job?" Now's a good time to do that. Are you overlooking skills that increase your marketability? As you work through the process, you'll be collecting the information you'll need to put together a dynamite resume. You'll have organized your thoughts to impress the interviewer of the value you will add to that organization. You'll be prepared to negotiate for a higher salary, more challenging work assignments and greater job satisfaction. You'll know a lot more about yourself and what makes you unique in the business world You'll see choices and take control of your destiny. Feeling good about your work (it's that attitude thing again) vastly impacts your quality of life.

The Monster of the Unknown
Fear and change

A key element of career planning is change. Our lifestyle needs change as our life experiences change. As a twenty-four-year-old right out of college, you may be much more interested in adventure than security, but as you settle into adulthood and gain the responsibilities that accompany it, your lifestyle needs change. The young truck driver married and had a family. Long distance driving was no longer fun, and he moved on. In the meantime he had traveled from Canada to Kentucky to New Jersey, and collected a paycheck the whole time.

Change by its very nature is stressful, to say the least. It requires you to make room in your life for new activities, to look at your life in new ways and to take risks. Fear of the unknown, or of change in general, can hold you back, even when you know odds are that change will be for the better. The biggest enemy for anyone who wants to change is inertia. Don't let it paralyze you into a lethargy that causes you to accept the status quo and prevents you from moving in new, and potentially more rewarding, directions. This discomfort is normal and necessary to the creative process. Accept that, and keep moving ahead, one small step at a time. Before long each small step adds up.

These chapters will help you overcome this natural reluctance. Each provides general information on a specific step in the process illustrated by a case study involving a real person, who, like yourself, used this system to take control of their professional life. (We've changed their names and some personal details to protect their privacy.) These are not casual meetings. You'll have a chance to walk in their shoes and to get to know them very well. You'll be able to identify with their situations, their concerns, their frustrations, their success. You'll see how to apply the theory and process to your own situation.

Taking stock of yourself is a most formidable task. It takes work, commitment, time and patience. It creates an invaluable data base, which gives you the power to pick and choose the interests, skills and values you want to pursue. But gathering this data doesn't have to take a lifetime. The exercises and inventories quickly give you a precise picture of who you are as a working professional; a picture of who you want to be. You are no longer a passive victim. You have taken control.

Becoming a Career Consumer
Learning Where to Shop

"Give a man a fish and he eats for a day. Teach him how to fish and he eats for a lifetime." Here you'll learn not only *how* to fish, but *where* to fish. As a career changer, you'll learn to determine employment trends within industries, forecast job security regionally and establish a way of thinking about your professional life that includes the entire world economy. In a world where car engines are made in Europe, the electronics are made in Asia, the body moldings and interiors are manufactured in Latin America and the automobiles are assembled in the United States, it is naive to assume you are not affected by the politics and economic climate of the entire world. As you develop your Professional Self, one of your most significant tasks will be to learn to receive, screen and interpret information in your role as a career consumer. It need not be difficult.

As you become more sophisticated in this role, you'll soon recognize industries and career paths likely to expand and those that are on a downward path. With this "macro economic" foundation in hand, and the information about yourself you've developed earlier, you'll be able to quickly eliminate unproductive areas. Once the elimination process is complete, what's left will direct you toward likely industries to concentrate on.

As you identify, research and review these industries, firms and positions, you'll develop your own criteria for benefits, organizational values and goals that are important to you. You'll find this particularly beneficial when you reach the negotiation stage.

Taking the Show on the Road
Marketing Yourself

Resumes and interviews are simply marketing tools to help you sell yourself. You are the one who gets the job. The fundamental techniques you'll find here groom you to present yourself as a competent, capable person. Developing these tools gives you the self-confidence you need to convince the employer you're worth what you're asking for.

Information is the key to unlocking your Professional Self and positioning yourself for the future you choose. You'll need not only information about yourself, the job market and the economy, but information on job search strategies and the career planning process. You open the door to new beginnings. Remember, the past cannot be changed but the future is whatever you want it to be.

> *You can now position yourself to achieve the future you choose.*

Each position you take in your professional life should provide you with the opportunity to learn new skills, challenge your existing ones and prepare you to move on.

> *To reach your goal, you must plan your future.*

Consciously setting up three- to five-year plans that develop guidelines for what you want to accomplish in that time will give you a road map to follow. This is not to suggest that in setting up these plans you will achieve all your goals. I've lived long enough to know that life has a way of taking unexpected turns and creating situations you could never expect or plan for. But it's surprising how often these plans work. A colleague of mine was the assistant director of alumni affairs at one of our California state colleges. Her first five-year plan called for her being appointed a director of alumni affairs within that time. She identified the skills and experience she felt were needed for that position, and set about acquiring them. After three years, the alumni affairs director unexpectedly accepted a new position at another school and she successfully applied for the job. She's now on her next

five-year-plan, to become director of development, and is building skills and experience in that direction.

As my colleague did, use your three- to five-year-plan to set
your goals. If you are able to achieve only half of what you set
out to do, think about all you'll have accomplished. And if you
don't, well, think about that too. If you don't set out a plan for
your life, who will?

Several years ago I asked a friend of mine, Sam Leer, a medical social worker who works with the terminally ill, to speak to
one of my classes. He encouraged my students to live their
dreams, to do what they wanted instead of always worrying about
what they should do.

"Nothing," he said, "is sadder than sitting with someone at
the end of their life and having them realize they have lived someone else's version of it."

Work should be an unending source of satisfaction, and here
you'll find the concrete steps you need to identify where to look
and what to look for to make this happen. Now you see your
Professional Self in total. You know who you are, you know what
you bring to the table, and you know what you want. You are
now in a power position. Use it.

Why Personal Assessment is So Important

- It identifies your Professional Self.

- It develops "raw data" for your job search.

- It enriches the vocabulary you use to describe your Professional Self.

- It lets you decide which skills, talents and traits you want to market, which you want to acquire, which you want to bank for another time, which you want to leave behind.

- Personal Assessment develops choices you never suspected you had.

2 Inventorying Your Interests
Integrate your interests with work

> *"You have the right to pursue meaningful work in an environment that is not only intellectually challenging, but in an area that you are drawn to."*

Jonathan Banks was a solitary man with a dull job who harbored a secret desire for excitement. He reminded me a little of a Woody Allen character, slight of build, shy, awkward and unassuming. He had always been a passive observer, content to sit back and let life happen to him. Now he wanted a change, but could not define, even to himself, what he wanted that change to be.

"I graduated from college in 1988 with a double major in music performance and mathematics. The two are not as disparate as they might seem," he answered my surprised expression. "Music is a very calculated kind of art made up of things like bars, notes, scales and measures."

When he left school he zeroed in on his math skills as his only employable option and was quickly hired by an insurance company as an actuary, computing insurance risks and premiums. His success was predictable, given his pedantic nature and he went on to get his certification.

"I'm twenty-eight-years old. I earned $72,000 last year. I've managed to accumulate a significant savings account, an attractive investment portfolio, and a great condo. I'm not really unhappy," he shrugged. "I just seem to be in a rut, and I want to get out. I want something more exciting. Working as an actuary is exceedingly independent work, there is little interaction with other people, and if I stay here, I'll never be involved with people."

"Is that a problem for you?" I asked.

"Actually, the real problem is that it's hard for me to make friends outside the office," he confessed. Now, five years into his career he found himself lonely as well as bored. He knew he needed to find the social interaction he craved in his work setting because his shy and retiring nature made it too difficult to generate this for himself during his leisure hours. ✳

A good place to begin defining your Professional Self is with your hobbies and special interests. Career changers should particularly look for opportunities to combine those interests, hobbies and talents with the job market to create a work experience that excites them.

Your work should stir you up. It's important when making career choices to think about what creates that stimulation for you. We all spend the majority of our adult lives involved in some sort of employment venture, so why not try to make it pleasurable? I'm always surprised at how few people do this, and amazed so many believe that work needs to be tedious, a drudgery, a bore.

You have the *right* to pursue meaningful work in an environment that is not only intellectually challenging but in an area that you are drawn to. You can and should include your outside interests and hobbies as you begin to explore employment opportunities.

One of my student clients demonstrates this profoundly. She was a national surfing champion who was graduating from our College of Creative Studies, where she had won several writing competitions. Faced with the need for a job, she couldn't seem to move ahead. Frustrated, I finally slammed my hand down on the table and demanded, "What is it you want?"

"You really want to know? I'm tired of school. All I want to do is hang out with surfers."

"All right. What skills do you have, aside from surfing, that are appropriate for that?" Because of her writing credentials, she began researching magazines. There are seventeen surfing magazines in this country, seven of them in California. Three invited her for interviews. She returned to me after one of them.

"This is the place for me! I got there at nine o'clock, but no one was there and the place was locked up. There was a sign on the door that said, 'Surf's up. Be back at noon.' That's my kind of place."

And sure enough, it was. But not forever. After two exciting years she was ready to move on. She earned her MBA at Stanford and today is Ms. Corporate America.

✳ *Although making a change was important to him, in his very measured way, Jonathan wanted to scientifically approach this career search so that he only had to make one switch. As Jonathan saw it, the way to do this was to get the help of a professional career counselor who would tell him what to do with the rest of his life. Not so! Career counselors can only guide. How successful Jonathan was depended on how willing he was to act on that guidance. I made no bones about that.*

"Have you thought about moving to a different industry that would provide you with a more interesting lifestyle?" I asked.

"I can certainly see myself using my mathematical skills and my computer skills, but to be an actuary you have to pretty much be in the insurance industry," he replied. Jonathan's attitudes about work were not negative so much as they were self-limiting.

Getting Jonathan to talk about what excited him was difficult. I kept trying to draw out what excited him, and initially he could think of very little, and he was very reticent to do any kind of testing.

"I've done these things before and I never know what to do with the results. It's just been a waste of time." ✳

Get Help from the Experts
The Strong Interest Inventory and What It Means

One way to define interest areas and relate them to job opportunities is through the Strong Interest Inventory (SII). The premise here is that people in a particular occupation usually have similar likes and dislikes, and how much they enjoy their

work comes from those interests and the relationships they develop with their co-workers. It stands to reason that if the people
you are working with have similar interests, likes and dislikes
you will be more likely to develop comfortable, compatible working relationships with them, and therefore get a greater degree of
satisfaction from your work. Career research has shown that
people often measure their "degree of satisfaction" about their
jobs by the quality of relationships or the people they work with.

The SII is based on six occupational themes as defined by
John Holland, author of *Making Vocational Choices* and one of the
internationally known experts on career development theory. The
inventory presents you with a series of activities, occupations,
and characteristics. You respond whether you like, dislike, or are
indifferent to them. Your replies are then compared to sets of
people in a number of occupations to determine compatibility. If
your responses are similar to, say, travel agents, you can assume
that you have a greater chance for job satisfaction within that particular occupation than in one where you had nothing in common.

Most career centers at community colleges and private career counselors offer this inventory and interpretation for nomi-
nal fees. If you don't have access to a career center or a career
counselor you can test yourself with Holland's Self-Directed
Search. Its easy and fun and comes with instructions for use and
interpretation. The test is published by Psychological Assessment Resources, Inc. (Call 1-800-331-TEST toll-free for information.) Or you can use the modified version, developed by Betty
Neville Michelozzi, included here.

The results of the SII are broken down into six occupational
themes: Realistic, Investigative, Artistic, Social, Enterprising, and
Conventional. Based on the results you are given a three letter
code which indicates the three occupational categories where you
were most compatible. For example, if your three strongest areas of compatibility were Investigative, Social and Enterprising,
your three letter code would be ISE.

✹ *"Standardized tests won't tell you what you should do," I told Jonathan. "It will give you and me a general direction from which to focus your occupational search. You initially told me you didn't want to experiment with a lot of different professions, you just wanted to make one decision and have that be a good decision," I reminded him. "Rather than asking you to try this and try that, let's take a look at what the SII indicates your areas of interest are going to be and then let's go with that. Let's begin to formulate a plan based on the information we get from this inventory. And if nothing else, we are going to find out what areas we can quickly cross off because you're not interested in them. What we want to find out is what kind of industries and what kind of work responsibilities are going to generate some measure of excitement for you," I said.*

When he returned the following week for an interpretation of the results, like many of my clients, he couldn't see the relevance of the results. Despite my disclaimers, he viewed this as an aptitude test and fully expected it would give him six or seven professions he would be "good" at. ✹

So many people say, "I took the SII and it said I should be a financial analyst," or a lawyer, or a whatever. The fact is, this inventory is not designed to identify *aptitude* or *competency*, but rather to identify occupational *interest* categories, indicating your compatibility with professionals in those occupations.

That's all.

The results do not indicate your talent, skill or experience with any of them, or that you have the necessary skills, but rather expands your avenues for further exploration. Look at the results of the SII as a road map that widens the highway as you move towards your career objectives.

When looking at your SII results, it is important to look at occupations in all of the themes of your code. This will give you the broadest variety of work environments, industries and positions to explore.

✹ *The three strongest occupational interest areas for Jonathan were Investigative, Artistic, and Conventional. This was not surprising to me. The Investigative fell right in line with his math background.*

Investigative types generally prefer to solve abstract problems and try to understand the physical world rather than act upon it.

The Artistic area validated his interest and love of music, and his aptitude and ability to perform in a musical environment. In college Jonathan had trained as a performance artist, but he chose not pursue this because of his shy, retiring temperament. He preferred to work alone, although he had a great need for individualistic expression and described himself as independent, original, and expressive.

As a direct opposite to these other two was the Conventional part of Jonathan that preferred highly ordered activities that he controlled. This again confirmed what we already knew about him. He did not like to be the leader, did not like to assume a tremendous amount of responsibility, liked to know exactly what was expected of him. He saw himself as conventional, stable, well-controlled and dependable. ✳

In establishing this base for yourself you are now in a position to determine what your next step is going to be, whether that is moving from one industry to another, looking more deeply into what you are already doing, or retraining to gain the necessary skills for a new occupation. Now that you have an idea of where to begin, you are better equipped to describe for yourself and others what kind of work you are looking for, in what industries, using what skills. Having an idea of where to begin feeds into greater self-confidence and control in the job search.

Next we looked at occupations that Holland defines as falling into the IAC categories, giving Jonathan a starting point for his occupational search. Investigative people prefer occupations like programmers, chemists, psychologists, mathematicians, science teachers, college professors and doctors. The Artistic types tend toward teaching English as well as art, interior decoration, photography, cosmetology, reporting, and advertising. Many of the Conventional type are happy as accountants, bankers, secretaries, credit managers, dietitians, and as business education teachers.

Visualizing Your Dream Job
Putting Fantasy to Work

Another way to home in on your passions is to visualize yourself in a new career. Concentrate on how it would be different from your current one.

✳ *To more clearly establish Jonathan's focus, we began talking about the actual work functions he saw himself doing.*

"Without any restrictions, without any basis in reality, give me what you think you'd want to do as a career," I challenged him. "You say you want excitement, you want a lifestyle change, what is it you think would be interesting to you?" This exercise was extremely difficult for Jonathan. He found himself unable to relax and open his mind up to creative thinking. ✳

If you're having trouble with this, try keying in on the hours of the day.

It's now eight o'clock in the morning. What are you doing? How is your day progressing? What are you involved with? What's happening around you? How are you dressed? What kind work environment are you in? What kind of work functions are you involved with? Do people come and ask you questions? What are you responsible for? Are you talking on the telephone? Are you in front of a computer? Describe what you see. What kind of industry do you see yourself in?

✳ *One of Jonathan's major complaints was the predictability of his present job. Getting up, going to work at eight and coming home at five, like clockwork, if you will. Now he saw himself still asleep at eight o'clock in the morning. He pictured himself waking up between ten and eleven and futsing around his condo, combining his household regimen with phone calls and other work related activities.*

"I am sick to death of my routine. I want to work where you sometimes have to stay until three or four in the morning, where there's deadlines and pressures and lots of people running around and you're wondering whether you're going to meet those deadlines. And somehow I

picture myself as this little satellite of calm amidst all this, doing my job and doing it well, but having all this activity going on around me. Right now I'm more interested in a lifestyle change than in making a lot of money. I can afford an entry level salary for a while, and I can always go back to being an actuary if I want to."

We began to work further with this fantasy. "What kind of industry do you see yourself in?" I asked him. He again pictured this chaos as someplace like a recording studio, or a place where music was produced, possibly music videos. He saw lots of young, energetic entertainers. I asked Jonathan to begin to explore some of the occupations found within the music industry.

He was reticent.

"How could I possibly earn a living in the music field when I'm not interested in being a musician myself? I understand it, I have a great deal of love for music, I play the guitar quite well, but I am not good enough to be a performance artist," he insisted. ✻

When you have dredged up all you possibly can from this exercise, consider the variety of occupations that industry requires. Search out people in these occupations and find out what they do and what it takes to do that. How do people break into this field? What education and experience will you need?

✻ One of the first tasks I assigned Jonathan was to look into different organizations or kinds of businesses within the recording industry, as you will learn to do in Chapter 6. He was surprised with the results. On the list he gave me, organized under three different aspects of the recording industry, were names of people who produced records, of talent agents who represented background singers, and of attorneys who specialized in entertainment law.

His next task was to learn about the culture of the industry. The letter requesting an informational interview you see in Chapter 7 resulted from his initial investigation. He now needed to sit down and talk to these people about what was involved. What were recording artists really like in the way they approached life's challenges? What are the day-to-day operations of a person who is a singer in a band? How are club dates made? How are recording contracts drawn up? How do you find backup singers? Who finds dancers to perform in your music videos? What's involved in the production of an album, a record, a compact disc? What are the technical differences in producing each of these? He needed to know all this and more if he was to figure out where his niche was.

Out of fifteen letters he sent out, three responded, and Jonathan began to exhibit an excitement I hadn't seen before. Although the thought of making appointments for these gave him goose bumps, he wanted the information, and once scheduled, he eagerly anticipated the meetings. He met with an entertainment lawyer, a talent agent, and a producer at Columbia Records. These three people each gave him the names of one or two others who did something a little bit different, but were still involved in the industry. Jonathan began to realize it was indeed possible to use his organizational and analytical skills in the music industry.

One of the areas he found attractive was that of personal manager to a recording artist. This seemed to dovetail with the skills that made him a successful actuary: organization, attention to detail and the ability to work on a variety of projects simultaneously.

"I see myself as the person who makes sure the hotel reservations are made, that gets the airline tickets, that makes sure the hotel has the proper diet and whatever else the artist needs and wants. I see myself as the one that makes sure the stage is set up properly." He saw himself keeping the artist's life uncluttered and free to concentrate on the creative demands of his profession. I watched Jonathan's excitement grow.

He began to see that he could take his lifelong interest in music and apply his technical skills in math and his organizational talents that came from his own self-management skills and involve himself in a very exciting industry that would give him the livelier lifestyle he craved.

"What if this doesn't meet your needs?" I asked Jonathan.

"If it doesn't, I'll look at some of the other areas I've uncovered. I never thought I could be involved in any of these simply because I was so focused on performance. Now I have a better appreciation of how many people it takes to bring that performance about. I know I can be one of them, even if I don't know exactly what that is right now."

It took the better part of a year before Jonathan made his change. One of the entertainment lawyers he had interviewed months earlier contacted him about an opening he'd heard about as personal manager for a rising rhythm and blues singer. Jonathan followed up and got the job as the "set up" man, the one who made sure everything was in order for each club date. He traveled extensively, and when he wasn't *on the road, he conducted his business from his condo. Last I heard, the first album was climbing the charts and it included one of Jonathan's original compositions.* ✳

As you gather more information you, too will realize it is indeed possible to use the skills and experience you have, or are willing to get, in the field of your passion. Go for it!

Personality/Interest Inventory

Circle the numbers of statements that clearly feel like something
you might say or do or think — something that feels like you.

1. It's important for me to have a strong, agile body.
2. I need to understand things thoroughly.
3. Music, color, beauty of any kind can really affect my moods.
4. People enrich my life and give it meaning.
5. I have confidence in myself that I can make things happen.
6. I appreciate clear directions so I know exactly what to do.
7. I can usually carry/build/fix things myself.
8. I can get absorbed for hours in thinking something out.
9. I appreciate beautiful surroundings; color and design mean a lot to me.
10. I love company.
11. I enjoy competing.
12. I need to get my surroundings in order before I start a project.
13. I enjoy making things with my hands.
14. It's satisfying to explore new ideas.
15. I always seem to be looking for new ways to express my creativity.
16. I value being able to share personal concerns with people.
17. Being a key person in a group is very satisfying to me.
18. I take pride in being very careful about all the details of my work.
19. I don't mind getting my hands dirty.
20. I see education as a lifelong process of developing and sharpening my mind.
21. I love to dress in unusual ways, to try new colors and styles.
22. I can often sense when a person needs to talk to someone.
23. I enjoy getting people organized and on the move.
24. A good routine helps me get the job done.
25. I like to buy sensible things I can make or work on myself.

26. Sometimes I can sit for long periods of time and work on puzzles or read or just think about life.
27. I have a great imagination.
28. It makes me feel good to take care of people.
29. I like to have people rely on me to get the job done.
30. I'm satisfied knowing that I've done an assignment carefully and completely.
31. I'd rather be on my own doing practical, hands-on activities.
32. I'm eager to read about any subject that arouses my curiosity.
33. I love to try creative new ideas.
34. If I have a problem with someone, I prefer to talk it out and resolve it.
35. To be successful, it's important to aim high.
36. I prefer being in a position where I don't have to take responsibility for decisions.
37. I don't enjoy spending a lot of time discussing things. What's right is right.
38. I need to analyze a problem pretty thoroughly before I act on it.
39. I like to rearrange my surroundings to make them unique and different.
40. When I feel down, I find a friend to talk to.
41. After I suggest a plan, I prefer to let others take care of the details.
42. I'm usually content where I am.
43. It's invigorating to do things outdoors.
44. I keep asking "why?"
45. I like my work to be an expression of my moods and feelings.
46. I like to find ways to help people care more for each other.
47. It's exciting to take part in important decisions.
48. I'm always glad to have someone else take charge.
49. I like my surroundings to be plain and practical.

50. I need to stay with a problem until I figure out an answer.
51. The beauty of nature touches something deep inside me.
52. Close relationships are important to me.
53. Promotion and advancement are important to me.
54. Efficiency, for me, means doing a set amount carefully each day.
55. A strong system of law and order is important to prevent chaos.
56. Thought-provoking books always broaden my perspective.
57. I look forward to seeing art shows, plays and good films.
58. I haven't seen you for so long; I'd love to know how you're doing.
59. It's exciting to influence people.
60. When I say I'll do it, I follow through on every detail.
61. Good, hard, physical work never hurt anyone.
62. I'd like to learn all there is to know about subjects that interest me.
63. I don't want to be like everyone else; I like to do things differently.
64. Tell me how I can help you.
65. I'm willing to take some risks to get ahead.
66. I like exact directions and clear rules when I start something new.
67. The first thing I look for in a car is a well-built engine.
68. These people are intellectually stimulating.
69. When I'm creating, I tend to let everything else go.
70. I feel concerned that so many people in our society need help.
71. It's fun to get ideas across to people.
72. I hate it when they keep changing the system just when I get it down.
73. I usually know how to take care of things in an emergency.
74. Just reading about new discoveries is exciting.
75. I like to create happenings.

76. I often go out of my way to pay attention to people who seem lonely and friendless.
77. I love a bargain.
78. I don't like to do things unless I'm sure they're approved.
79. Sports are important in building strong bodies.
80. I've always been curious about the way nature works.
81. It's fun to be in a mood to try or do something unusual.
82. I believe that people are basically good.
83. If I don't make it the first time, I usually bounce back with energy and enthusiasm.
84. I appreciate knowing exactly what people expect of me.
85. I like to take things apart to see if I can fix them.
86. Don't get excited. We can think it out and plan the right move logically.
87. It would be hard to imagine my life without beauty around me.
88. People often seem to tell me their problems.
89. I can usually connect with people who get me in touch with a network of resources.
90. I don't need much to be happy.

Scoring Your Answers

To score, circle the same numbers below that you circled on the preceding pages.

R	I	A	S	E	C
1	2	3	4	5	6
7	8	9	10	11	12
13	14	15	16	17	18
19	20	21	22	23	24
25	26	27	28	29	30
31	32	33	34	35	36
37	38	39	40	41	42
43	44	45	46	47	48
49	50	51	52	53	54
55	56	57	58	59	60
61	62	63	64	65	66
67	68	69	70	71	72
73	74	75	76	77	78
79	80	81	82	83	84
85	86	87	88	89	90

Now add up the number of circles in each column:
R _4_ I _9_ A _11_ S _10_ E _11_ C _8_

Which are your three highest scores:
1st _____A_____ 2nd _____E_____ 3rd _____S_____

Holland's Occupational Themes
Typical characteristics

Realistic: Practical, active and have good physical skills. Someone who enjoys working outside and creating things with their
hands. Prefer to deal with things rather than ideas or people.
Sometimes has difficulty expressing ideas in words or in communicating feelings to others. Political and economic ideas are fairly
conventional.

Typical occupations:
Athletic trainer
Forester
Radiology technician
Police officer
Military services
Electrician
Architect
Engineer
Carpenter

Investigative: Prefers to solve abstract problems and understand
the physical world rather than acting upon the world. Enjoys
complicated problems and intellectual challenges. Tends not to
like structured situations, lots of rules, or working around many
people.

Typical occupations:
Computer programmer
Medical professions
Chemist
Pharmacist
Psychologist
Mathematician

Science teacher
Systems analyst

Artistic: Prefers unstructured situations where problems are dealt with through self expression in the artistic media. Prefers to work alone, has a great need for individualistic expression, and is sensitive and emotional. Would describe themselves as independent, original, unconventional, expressive and energetic.

Typical occupations:
Art teacher
Interior decorator
Photographer
Cosmetologist
Reporter
Public relations director
Advertising
English teacher

Social: Sociable, responsible, humanistic and concerned with the welfare of others. Express themselves well and get along well with others. Like to be near the center of groups and prefer to solve problems by discussing them with others. See themselves as cheerful, popular, achieving and as good leaders.

Typical occupations:
Public school administrator
Guidance counselor
Recreation leader
Social worker
Occupational therapist
Speech pathologist
Elementary school teacher

Enterprising: Has great facility with words which they put to effective use in selling and leading. Enjoys persuading others to their viewpoints and are impatient with work involving precision or long periods of intellectual concentration. See themselves as energetic, enthusiastic, adventurous, self-confident and dominant.

> ### Typical occupations:
> Restaurant manager
> Travel agent
> Buyer
> Marketing executive
> Personnel director
> Investment manager
> Store manager
> Realtor
> Dental hygienist

Conventional: Prefers highly ordered activities, does not like to be a leader and likes working in a well-established chain of command. Likes to know exactly what is expected of them and feels uncomfortable when they don't know the "rules." See themselves as conventional, stable, well-controlled and dependable.

> ### Typical occupations:
> Accountant
> Banker
> Secretary
> Credit manager
> Dietitian
> Dental assistant
> Business education teacher

3 Identifying Your Skills
Don't overlook the obvious

> *"Until you begin to look at the skills you have and how they empower you, you may find it difficult to believe in yourself."*

In my work with clients I am constantly bombarded by remarks ranging from "I have nothing to offer an employer, I have no skills," to "All I know how to do is this one job. How can I possibly change careers if this is all I know how to do?" It's almost as if they wish to categorize accomplishments as irrelevant before a potential employer has the chance to do it for them. Many of us go through life wearing these blinders. Thirty percent of college students strongly believe their first *job* defines their *career*, according to according to Phil Gardner, Collegiate Employment Research Institute.

To make my point, try this. Look at the following sentence.

> *"Feature films are the result of years of scientific study combined with the experience of years."*

How many *f's* are there in the statement? Do you see two? three? five? No cheating. Did you come up with six? If you didn't, go back and see if you can find them all now.

As you can see, all too often we overlook the obvious. As you begin your own personal assessment you may run into the same problem. Overlooking the obvious. It's time to throw away your blinders.

A colleague of mine says success comes in "cans." That means taking the "'t" off can't. Success comes as a result of an attitude of: "Yes I can! I *can* and *will* take charge of my career!" Another wise sage said, "Act enthusiastic and you'll be enthusiastic."

Employers will judge experiences according to their own criteria. Your job is to show how the skills and experiences you already have prepare you for this position, to sell yourself as a qualified person for this particular opening. Defining those skills is a challenging venture.

✳ *Pat Erickson was a good example of that.*

"I need help in writing a resume," she announced upon entering my office.

"Why is that?" I asked, waving her to a chair.

"I've applied for a promotion to assistant buyer."

I nodded.

"No, you don't understand," she insisted. "I have to get this job. I can't just apply for it, I must get this job."

I asked for some background.

Until 40, she had been a career wife and mother. During her 20-year marriage she had successfully raised two children and was well known for her community involvement. Her husband, Ted, a union laborer working in the mining industry, made good money, but they had worked hard to raise a family on just one salary. Both valued Pat's involvement in their children's education and in the community, and by careful management, they had built up a modest savings.

"The trouble started in the summer of 1985," she explained. Hard times hit the mining industry in which Ted had spent his working life. The company announced layoffs.

"We weren't particularly concerned in the beginning. This had happened before. We would just wait out this storm as we had the others."

Only this time was different. The layoff lasted three and a half years.

At the end of the first year, the Eriksons faced the fact that Ted could not rely on being rehired in the foreseeable future.

"That's when I began thinking about going to work." It was frightening. The mine was the major employer in the community and the

layoffs affected the entire job market. There were few jobs, period. Pat was also uncertain about what she was capable of doing because she had never worked for a paycheck.

"I'd never done anything," she told me. "I'd never supported anyone, I'd never worked for anyone."

In desperation Pat applied for and got a job at a tortilla factory located about five miles from her home, as an ordinary laborer on the assembly line at minimum wage. While the tortilla factory was still a family owned and operated enterprise, it was a large company, employing hundreds of people in an industry grossing in the millions of dollars annually.

"I learned the job in the first week, met my quotas the second, and was bored by the third," she recalled. While her creative mind rebelled against the tediousness of the work, she recognized it for what it was – a job, and her family desperately needed the income.

"But it wasn't long before I realized minimum wage wasn't enough to support my family." Something had to be done.

As she patiently fed tortillas into the oven, she pondered the problem. She liked the company, felt comfortable there, she admitted, and determined that it was a new position, not a new company she needed. Her enterprising intellect began cataloging the other jobs around her and she began to think about what else she could do. She felt uncomfortable about her lack of experience, but she needed to make more money. Necessity, the mother of all motivators, pushed her to look more aggressively at what might be available.✻

According to Richard Bolles, author of the legendary *What Color is Your Parachute,* the average college graduate has at his disposal a range of between eight hundred and two thousand potentially marketable skills. As we gain work and life experiences our "skills bank" should increase accordingly. In developing a career plan for yourself, you must be able to recognize the skills you have already mastered from all aspects of your life.

Start by understanding there are different kinds of skills and some of them are not always acquired through education or training. Sometimes skills are natural tendencies or personality traits, sometimes they are skills you developed through hobbies and interests and sometimes they are job related skills. These skills are yours to do with as you wish. You can store them away to be used at a later date or you can use them every day.

> ✱*"Last week I noticed an open position as an assistant buyer. I figured all my life I've been buying things, and on a very restrictive budget," she told me. "It was payday. I looked at my check and made the decision to apply."*
>
> *The job was on a paraprofessional level, and required a resume. She had never done this. That's when she came to see me.*
>
> *"Why do you feel you're qualified to be an assistant buyer?" I asked.*
>
> *"Because all my life I've bought things," she reiterated. "Up until now Ted's always made good money, but we've only had one income and so I had to be quite frugal in my purchases. The position calls for a buying assistant. I would just be buying different things in greater quantity."*
>
> *I pointed out that her reasoning was somewhat naive. I could see her confidence deflate, but just for an instant. She straightened herself up in the chair, set her jaw, and said again, "I need this job." ✱*

There are three commonly accepted categories of skills loosely defined as:

Functional skills, which can be transferred to and implemented in many different interest areas and work settings. Some of these are: supervising, delegating, organizing, communicating, evaluating, presenting.

The ten hottest transferable skills, according to noted career change counselor Howard Figler, are budget management, supervising, public relations, coping with deadline pressure, negotiating/arbitrating, speaking, writing, organizing/managing/coordinating, interviewing, and teaching/instructing. These "soft skills" are mainly acquired through experience rather than formal training. They are less easy to recognize since they tend to be linked to dealing with processes rather than doing things. Some samples are given at the end of the chapter. Do keep in mind that functional skills will not substitute for technical skills.

Technical skills reflect your ability to perform the tasks associated with a specific occupation or profession. These "hard skills" are easy to recognize since they are often identified as "qualifications" for specific jobs. These are skills you learn in school, in a training program or on the job. Examples are: engineering, bookkeeping, computer skills, word processing, accounting, graphic design, translating, counseling. These skills tend to be associated with specific tasks or job functions and are often harder to transfer from one field to another.

Personal management (sometimes called adaptive skills) reflect your ability to get along smoothly with others in work settings and to manage different stresses on the job as well as in other areas of your life. Some of these are: analytical, logical, independent, diplomatic, conscientious, motivated, dependable, adaptable and easy to get along with. According to the National Association of Colleges and Employers (NACE), the number one reason people are discharged is their inability to work and get along with their co-workers.

Communicating Your Assets
Developing a Skills Vocabulary

Your first step is to develop a vocabulary for describing skills in general. One of the most difficult parts of the job search is the development of this professional vocabulary. To get a handle on it, take a blank sheet of paper and a pencil and write down all 26 letters of the alphabet on the left hand side of the page. Take three minutes. As quickly as you can, write down an adjective or action verb that begins with each of the letters of the alphabet. This exercise stimulates your brain to think of words to help you articulate your skills. These words also come in handy later as you prepare your resume and get ready for interviews.

You may get stuck at first, but keep trying. Remember you are in the process of learning a new skill and it will feel awkward at first.

Here's a sample of the kinds of words you might think about and begin to incorporate into your own career mind set.

A ...... Adapted
B .... Budgeted
C ...... Communicated
D ...... Developed
E .... Evaluated
F .... Filed
G ...... Generated
H ...... Hired
I .... Investigated
J .... Juggled
K ...... Kept
L .... Lead
M ..... Managed
N ...... Negotiated
O ...... Operated
P .... Persuaded
Q ...... Qualified
R ...... Researched
S .... Supervised
T .... Translated
U ...... Utilized
V ...... Verbalized
W ..... Wrote
X ...... Xeroxed
Y ...... Yield
Z .... Zany

Make a new list every day for a week. By the end of the week you should be able to comfortably list words for at least 24 out of the 26 letters. I'll give you a break with x and z, and you might have a little difficulty with are k, j and q, too. The rest should begin to come more easily with practice. Try to come up with different words every day you do this exercise, and be sure to keep your lists. Now apply those words to your own life experience. Learn not to trivialize your assets, but think about contexts in which they have been useful. Then break them down into functional, technical and personal management skills.

    ✱ *"I don't have time for this," Pat objected.*
    "Yes, you do. The job doesn't close for two more weeks. When you bring these back you'll be amazed at what we will have to work with."
    Equipped with her seven lists of words, Pat returned the next week.
    On three separate sheets of paper Pat broke down her skills into each of the skill areas. Some did not fit exactly into any of the categories but I asked her to pick the one that came closest. ✱

    This kind of self-assessment is often revealing. Think of it as creating a shopping list of your assets: your interests, learned skills, natural aptitudes and your work-related achievements and experiences; something you can do as well as, or better than, most people. It isn't easy. It takes dedicated practice. Begin by focusing on your successes and achievements and what brought them about, and it will get easier as you go along.

    There is an extra benefit to this exercise. The process of skills identification and developing a skills inventory involves the issue of choice, giving you the power to decide which skills you will use on your new job. If you decide that a skill you have mastered is one you don't want to use on your next job, it's your choice not to include it. Just because you are very good at something doesn't mean that you have to use it in your next job. I know a woman who is experienced in machine repairs, such as typewriters, copiers, PCs and the like. This is a well paid skill that is in demand, but she chooses not to pursue it. "I don't want to spend the rest of my life in work pants, carrying around a tool kit."

Search through your work and education history. Select out of that bag what you want to carry to your next job, those to bank for future use, those you will have to acquire in order to achieve the level of employment you're seeking, and those to leave behind. The choice is yours.

For instance, the secretary who can assess her true skills may find she is actually doing the work of an office manager and purchasing agent. The teacher who has brought in thousands of dollars in grant money may realize she has skills as a fund-raiser. A loan officer probably has marketing and analytical skills. A volunteer who has done public relations work for her church or women's organization can often transfer those skills to paid employment.

Log on to Your Current Skills
Dissecting Your Past

Another way to develop a skills list is to keep a log of your job duties. Focus on what you do on a daily basis or what you've done in the past. Think about the skills you use to perform each task.

Another way of uncovering your skills is to take a specific experience, one you remember in vivid detail, one you are especially proud of, and in which you played an active role. This can be something you did while working, something you achieved through involvement with community or social groups, or maybe something that improved your family's home life. Focus on those things that are of paramount importance to the employer–those activities and accomplishments that the employer perceives to be important to the organization's long-term strategic goals.

Employers also want to know about leadership, taking responsibility for a project, setting a goal and bringing together the people and resources to achieve that goal.

✳ *Thinking back over her career as a mother, Pat identified her PTA involvement as her most significant experience.*

While she had held leadership positions throughout the years, her most spectacular accomplishment came with her first dive into the water. When her children were in the second and third grades and she realized they needed help in developing their reading skills. Too bad there were no reading labs in the schools, the teachers told her. A private tutor was beyond her means. Believing there were other families in the same predicament, she brought this up at the next PTA meeting. As organizations of this kind are wont to do, she was told, "If this is important to you, why don't you take the ball and run with it?"

Accepting the challenge, she recruited three other mothers whose children also had reading difficulties and together they approached the school board at one of its regularly scheduled meetings and asked why there were no reading labs. The board was sympathetic to their concerns, but pointed out it had been unable to get these labs funded. Pat asked what needed to be done and was told a grant proposal needed to be written thoroughly documenting the need with supporting material, including a budget, program development and implementation, control systems, and evaluation of results. It sounded overwhelming, and I'm sure the board never expected to hear from Pat or her committee again.

Nevertheless, the creation of the reading labs was important, so Pat broke the project down into specific tasks and assigned one to each of the women on her committee. One was to learn the process for writing a grant. She assigned another to collect the documentation of need by contacting other parents whose children were in the same age group . The other was to gather signatures for support of the reading labs. Pat took on the budget preparation. All these were bite-sized pieces that each worked on individually over the next few months. They met weekly to discuss their progress.

As the project began to take more shape and purpose, Pat began to see the need for expert advice.

She recontacted the superintendent's office to ask for information and assistance. She found she got better response when she put her requests in writing. I pointed out that this required communication skills. She was getting her needs across to other people who in turn were answering her requests. She was also making sure that there was communication all up and down the line, from the school board to the PTA to herself and her committee.

When it came time to present the findings to the school board, the group appointed her to make the presentation. By using charts and graphs made at her kitchen table, she clearly documented the need, presented a budget that seemed workable, and talked about alternative budgets in terms of cost saving measures. She kept the presentation to just under an hour and provided enough convincing material that the project received the necessary approval for proposal development. A professional grant writer, employed by the school district, was assigned to work with the women on the formal proposal, which was also approved and funded. The final grant affected not just Pat's school and her children, but the entire district. ✳

Don't overlook your volunteer experience. Look at your unpaid efforts as meaningful work experience. Employers will pay attention to these activities, but only if you are capable of articulating their significance to the position at hand. They are especially interested if you prepared an annual budget, edited or wrote a newsletter, designed advertising flyers, held office, organized conferences and other meetings, or raised funds, but you must be able to articulate their significance to the position. For instance, Anne Sweeney was a flight attendant who sought and won a corporate communications job. One of the reasons she could make this transition was that she had produced newsletters while a flight supervisor. She also was considered to have labor-relations experience because she had been her fellow flight attendants' union representative – also an unpaid job.

Realize that often the things that are most important to us are the things we learn from the most and have the best chance at a professional payoff. One example is Cathy Thompson, a former junior high school art teacher, who volunteered for fund raising projects and assisted participants at a therapeutic facility for the handicapped where her son was enrolled. The center's assistant director recognized her commitment and eventually encouraged her to apply for the full-time, paid position of volunteer coordinator. In this position she was responsible for recruiting, hiring and training a staff of eight hundred volunteers, writing press releases and handling all of the center's publicity.

"Volunteering was a good way for me to learn a new business because of the hands-on training," she says. "And even though I didn't earn a salary, it definitely paid off down the road."

Try writing down your most memorable experience. Describe your part in it. It may take you several paragraphs or two or three pages depending on the degree of detail you recall from the experience. Don't rush. Linger over the memory. Is there anything else that needs to be recalled?

Responsibilities + Skills = Accomplishments
Add Meaning to Your Skills

Once you are comfortable that you have remembered as much as you can of this experience, take your script and use the action verbs, adjectives and descriptors you developed to articulate it in terms of the skills required.

If you have been a student or career wife and mother, you'll draw most heavily on your volunteer skills. If you have formal work experience, you want to categorize the skills you're now using or have acquired in past positions. Describe in detail your duties. Next begin to attach skills to those duties and then think about the accomplishments of the activity. For each activity you dissect, ask yourself:

- What did the activity involve? (Responsibilities)
- What did it take to accomplish those responsibilities?(Skills)
- What was the result? (Accomplishments)

This will enable you to describe your skills in concise, unambiguous terms; back up your claims by referring to actual experiences in your life, and make a clear connection between your skills and the needs of the employer.

✻ We began with a hard look at Pat's job description. The major duty was to assist the buyer in the requisitioning and purchasing of staples for the tortillas, but the job required several additional skills: organizational skills, some writing, and communication and account- ability skills.

As we began to explore and identify the skills she possessed, her confidence resurfaced.

I pointed out that she acted in a supervisory capacity because she controlled the reading labs project. She took responsibility for it and she segregated and delegated the tasks that needed to be done. Making sure that each of her team stayed on track was again a man- agement responsibility. She also provided the necessary nurturing and encouragement that kept them willing and able to work on the project. She had used creative and analytical skills when she conceived ways to get the required materials, components, and services in a cost effective manner. She had negotiated prices, terms, and schedules with ven- dors in order to develop the budget she submitted, a key skill for the job she was now after. She had used oral communication in delivering her presentation, and written communication in clarifying the information she needed in order to make the initial presentation and then the formal grant proposal. And most important, the results of Pat's efforts were documented.

Pat could now see that her PTA experience had given her budget- ing experience, communication skills, supervisory skills, management skills, and the ability to keep people on track and working toward the same goal, all of which correlated to the qualifications outlined in the job description for the assistant buyer. Pat was able to take what she saw as a basically "homemaker" situation and turn it into an experience that clearly demonstrated the kinds of skills required by the job she was after. She was able to break her skills down by the components re- quired for the new position. She was able to tell her employers that she had developed the requirements of the job over a long period of time, and that she used these skills on a consistent basis. What she had done could be effectively put to work in planning and securing large scale purchases and working effectively with vendors to meet the needs of her company. They believed her and offered her the job. ✻

Until you begin to look at the skills you have and how they empower you, you may also find it difficult to believe in yourself as worthy of the confidence you want your new employer to place in you. By getting to know the skills you already have in hand, you can use this confidence to take a greater degree of control over your career search.

✻ After seven months her supervisor was promoted to another position and Pat was again interviewed. Based primarily on her performance and her ability to articulate the new skills she had acquired, management offered her the buyer's position. She continued to grow with the company and to develop and apply more skills. The last time I saw her, she was so excited she could hardly wait to get the social preliminaries out of the way.

"You'll never guess what," she blurted immediately. "My Business and Professional Women's chapter just named me 'Woman of the Year!'"✻

Constant practice of this process will make it routine. The operative word is "practice." With practice and reinforcement, I guarantee the results will improve your self-esteem and give you a better understanding of your Professional Self. Psychologists believe it takes twelve weeks of daily reinforcement in order for anything to become a habit and become incorporated into your routine, so be persistent. Get started now. You may discover a new you hiding behind the obvious.

Skill Classifications

Below is a sample of skills and their applications based on the work of Paul Breen and Urban Whitaker in consultation with students, faculty members and employers in the humanities and behavioral and social sciences. As you identify your skills, think of the situations where you used them, and what resulted.

Information Management Skills involve the ability to:
> Sort data and objects.
> Apply information creatively to specific problems or tasks.
> Understand and use organizing principles.
> Evaluate information against appropriate standards.
> Synthesize facts, concepts and principles.

Valuing Skills involve the ability to:
> Assess a course of action in terms of its long-range effects on general human welfare.
> Make decisions that will maximize both individual and collective good.

Communication Skills involve the ability to:
> Listen with objectivity and paraphrase the content of a message.
> Use various forms and styles of written communication.
> Speak effectively to individuals and groups.
> Use media formats to present ideas imaginatively.
> Express one's needs, wants, opinions and preferences without offending the sensitivities of others.

Research and Investigation Skills involve the ability to:
> Identify information sources appropriate to special needs or problems.
> Apply a variety of methods to test the validity of data.

Identify problems and needs.

Design an experiment, plan or model that systematically defines a problem.

Formulate questions relevant to clarifying a particular problem, topic or issue.

Critical Thinking Skills involve the ability to:

Identify quickly and accurately the critical issues when making a decision or solving a problem.

Identify a general principle that explains interrelated experiences or factual data.

Identify reasonable criteria for assessing the value or appropriateness of an action or behavior and apply to strategies and action plans.

Adapt one's concepts and behavior to changing conventions and norms.

Create innovative solutions to complex problems.

Analyze the interrelationships of events and ideas from several perspectives.

Design and Planning Skills involve the ability to:

Identify alternative courses of action.

Assess needs and set realistic goals and priorities.

Follow through with a plan or decision.

Manage time effectively.

Predict future trends and patterns.

Accommodate multiple demands of time energy and resources.

Management and Administration Skills involve the ability to:

Motivate and lead people.

Identify resource materials useful in the solution of a problem.

Delegate responsibility for the completion of a task.

Human Relations and Interpersonal Skills involve the ability to:

Keep a group "on track" and moving toward the achievement of a common goal.

Use argumentation techniques to persuade others.

Make commitments to persons.

Be willing to take risks.

Teach a skill, concept or principle to others.

Work under time and environment pressures.

Personal and Career Development Skills involve the ability to:

Analyze and learn from life experiences – both one's own and others.

Relate the skills developed in one environment to the requirements of another.

Persist with a project when faced with failure.

Recognize when a project cannot be carried out or is not worth the effort required to complete it.

Generate trust and confidence in others.

4 Determining Your Work Values
Setting priorities

> *"Values are the emotional salary of work."*

We usually think of careers as vehicles for achieving material well-being, psychological growth and personal fulfillment, but as human beings we have additional spiritual and altruistic needs: the desire for a rewarding purpose, the need to be meaningfully related to the rest of humanity, and the desire to use one's talents in the service of others.

Howard Figler, author of the classic *The Complete Job-Search Handbook*, takes this one step further.

"Your selection of one particular kind of work from among the thousands available must reflect what you regard as important, worth doing, inherently valuable." He describes values as the "emotional salary of work." Look at work values as attitudinal measuring sticks for determining your most important sources of satisfaction, be that working with disabled people, dancing, growing plants, involving yourself in social change, making decisions with numbers, or selling ideas.

These broad themes are sometimes referred to as "unifying principles," golden nuggets of truth used as a guide for goal planning and living. When what you do is congruent with what you value, you achieve the best form of personal productivity and your self-esteem soars. Today's typical career path is like a series of crossroads. At each junction you must decide to go in one

direction and not another. Change is risky, but it can be a rewarding venture. Ask yourself: What is there in my life that I
value, and what is missing from it? The answers give you direction. Facing up to this question may be frightening at the outset,
but this fear is no reason to delay getting on with it. With all the
time and energy you spend at work, being fulfilled from Monday
to Friday is a large measure of how happy you are with life in
general. I often see people who are successful in their careers but
are unhappy because they get no "emotional salary" from their
work. You can avoid that.

Begin by identifying your values in relation to how you live
your life, how you feel about work and how you relate to other
people. These contribute to your sense of self-worth as much as
to a stable career path. An incomplete awareness of your values
can lead you to make conflicting choices that you later regret. If
the changes you make in your life reflect your deeply felt goals
and desires, the natural stress that accompanies them will be minimal and can even be positive.

Your reassessment doesn't have to result in a drastic change
of direction. Sometimes a shift in emphasis – maybe incorporating more client contact into your job, or working with a team of
people you really respect and enjoy – is all it takes to customize
your current position. Other times a complete career overhaul is
needed.

＊ *This was Sara Miller's dilemma when a career change was thrust
upon her.*

*In the beginning it was frightening. The pain, the numbness, the
swelling in her hands and arms as her capable fingers manipulated the
dental tools was excruciating, and it occurred more and more often.
Diagnosis: Carpal Tunnel Syndrome, an ailment common to people
who perform repetitive tasks and quick movements with their hands
over a period of time. The specialists and the rehabilitation counselor
agreed. An operation could relieve her pain, but the ultimate cure was
to leave the profession that aggravated the problem.*

Cold fear gripped her stomach. Her children depended upon her. Could she afford to change?

Gradually the panicky feeling subsided, pushed aside as she mulled the possibilities of new challenges, only to surface again as the mortgage payment came due.

"I know I'm capable. I know I have skills. I just don't seem to be able to figure out where a retired dental hygienist takes her marbles to find a new game," she told me.

I could understand her concern. Initially Sara said she wanted her next career to be something that was more prestigious than the last. Her big fear was that she was going to have to sacrifice her income to do that. ✳

The realities of career change often require an income reduction. You may have a position of responsibility you have worked hard to achieve, which compensates you for that accomplishment. When enterting a new field, you will probably start at the bottom. You need to think about how important this is to you. Think about the long-term as well. Will you be happy at this five, ten years from now? And if the difference is too much, that's okay. You haven't burned any bridges or locked yourself into anything yet.

Another reality is that you may need retraining in order to achieve your highest values. This might mean adding a degree, earning a certificate, qualifying for a license, or gaining experience in the field through internships and training programs.

✳*We briefly discussed Sara's options, among them retraining. She was adamant.*

"I'm not interested in going back to school. I don't want to take the time, and I don't have the energy. Besides, I need something right now, not two years down the road." She would have to take her experience and parlay that into a new career. So we moved on from there.

To start with, we looked at what she especially liked about being a dental hygienist.

"First was the money," she acknowledged. "I earned up to $200 a day depending on the number of bookings I arranged. I made somewhere around $35,000 a year, not bad for a woman without a college

degree, is it?" She and her children lived quite comfortably and she was proud of that.

She had contracted independently with several local dentists and found she liked this flexibility. It allowed her to work around her children's needs and school schedules. She also liked the leisure time this flexibility afforded her.

"I liked the idea of helping others. I liked feeling I made a difference in people's lives.

On the downside was lack of security.

"Look at me right now." As an independent agent, when she was unable to see clients because she was ill, she lost that income.

Because she contracted with five different dentists in town, no one claimed her, there was no sense of loyalty to her and she missed that.

"It's basically the same kind of function on a day-to-day basis," she complained. This had caused her disability in the first place, the tediousness of the job, the continuousness of the tasks.

She was especially dissatisfied at the lack of prestige she perceived the profession commanded.

"People see dental hygienists as just janitors of the mouth. When the dentist is done with all the technical work that makes the mouth function, then the dental hygienist comes in and does the cleanup work," she said.

"People take for granted what I do," she continued. "There is never any feedback on my performance. Patients don't have any idea of what's going on when their mouths are open and they're staring up into the light. Once you've established yourself, dentists very seldom come in and check your work," she explained. "You have to develop your own sense of positive reinforcement." ✳

Discovering What You Want
Values Clarification

To help clarify what you want in your next career, complete the values clarification exercise you will find at the end of the chapter. The exercise asks you to rate the importance of each of the following work values on a scale of one to eight, with eight being highest: High Income, Prestige, Independence, Helping

Others, Security, Variety, Leadership, Working in Your Main Field of Interest, Leisure, Challenge, Interpersonal Relations and Creativity. (See the exercise for precise definitions of these values.)

There are two parts to the exercise. You'll need two copies of the Value Scale. For the first part, fill out the first scale in terms of how you feel about your current work. Then do the same in the second column for what you want in your next career.

✱ *Sara took the exercise home with her, and returned the next day. She found conflicting responses in the areas of Prestige, Security, Variety, Leadership, Challenge and Creativity, pinpointing facets she wanted to change.* ✱

When You Can't Have Everything
Looking at Choices

One of the most difficult things for people to accept when launching a new career search is the necessity of compromise. In order to be happy with the compromises you do make, you must first establish what is really important in your life. Then you can decide what you are willing to give up to achieve that.

To determine which of these values you've just identified command your highest priority and which were really just "nice to have," total your Initial Score column on your second copy of the scale.

The crux of this exercise is to achieve an exact score of forty-eight. If the total exceeds this score, you must go back to each value and adjust or eliminate the original scores so that the total comes down to no more than forty-eight. The adjusted scores are entered in the second column. This "Adjusted Score" then reflects those values about which you feel strongest. (If the total is less than forty-eight, you aren't off the hook. You must adjust and add until you reach the magic number. It's the forced choice that really tests and confirms your values.)

My clients sometimes do this exercise two or three times throughout our sessions together. Each time, as their values become clearer and they verbalize them better, they get closer to a precise idea of what is essential to them.

✳ *On the scale for what she wanted in her next career, Sara gave High Income, Variety, Leadership and Prestige each a seven. She gave Independence, Security, Challenge and Creativity a six. Working in Your Main Field of Interest and Interpersonal Relationships scored fours, while she only gave Leisure and Helping Others threes. This totaled sixty-six points, almost twenty points over the maximum. She had to eliminate 18 eighteen points in order to get to the required limit.*

During Sara's second pass with the Values Scale, it was interesting to watch her process of elimination.

"I need a good income, but if I relocated to a less expensive area, I could probably get by on less than I have been, especially if the job had good potential down the road." So she changed her answer from a seven to a five.

Prestige was very important to her and she was only willing to give up one point of that. She still felt strongly about Independence, that she needed some control over her schedule to accommodate her children, but that it wasn't as much a factor if she relocated to someplace like Seattle where her family lived, so she switched that to a four.

"After my divorce I considered moving back there," she explained. "I decided against it then because I knew it would be difficult to reestablish my practice where no one knew me. It would be different now. I don't have that problem. My folks are getting older, and my children have never been around an extended family. The cost of living is a good deal less than here. If I had to take a cut in income, it would certainly go a lot farther there."

Helping Others went from a three to a one.

"My whole life reflects my interest in helping others, from Cub Scouts, to after school programs, and reading for the blind. I've always done these things and I expect I will continue. I don't feel I need this kind of fulfillment in my job."

She was non-negotiable around the issue of Security.

"Maybe I can get along on less money, but I have to have a dependable base salary and I can grow from there."

*Another important point was that she wanted some sense of iden-
tification with, of belonging to, an organization. She was not willing to
negotiate on that.*

*Variety was important. The repetitiousness of her former job cre-
ated the need for a new career. She didn't want to fall into that trap
again. She went from a seven to a six and wasn't willing to go beyond
that. She decided to bump Leadership from a seven to a five.*

*"When you start a new profession you can't expect you're going
to be in a position to assume a leadership role. I know I'll prove myself
in time and then I can expect to move into a leadership role."*

*She dropped the Interest field to a one because she believed she
wanted to stay within the health care industry, so she didn't need to
waste any points for that. She was becoming very, very stingy with her
points.*

*She kept Leisure at a three because she still felt she needed to
have time with her children. She changed Challenge by one point, reasoning that the challenge had been thrust upon her and there was no
need to actively go out and pursue it.*

*She reduced Interpersonal Relations by only one point, from a
four to a three, because she felt she needed to look at a profession that
was people oriented. As a dental hygienist she felt she had little opportunity to interact with people on a social level.*

*"People don't talk to you much while your hands are in their
mouths."*

*Again she felt there were other avenues, other outlets for her Cre-
ativity and she dropped that to a four.*

The second total came within one point of the goal of forty-eight.

*"Oh, boy. Now what do I do? I've already compromised as far as
I can."*

*I held her to the task. It is important to take that last step. She
finally struck through the number for Interpersonal Relations and moved
that to a two.*

*"If I have to give up something, it will have to be the people orien-
tation. I've done that before, I guess I can do it again."*

*This would not mean her job wouldn't be people oriented, only
that this wouldn't be uppermost in her criteria as she looked for careers.*

*As she worked and reworked this exercise it became dramatically
apparent that in the final analysis her highest values were Prestige, Security and Variety. She could now take a look at potential careers with*

these in mind. The areas of compromise were Independence, High Income, Leadership, Challenge and Interest Field because she felt all those would come as a result of the new profession.

Now that Sara was clear on her own values, she needed to use this information to analyze her opportunities. ✳

Smell the Coffee
Wishing Doesn't Make It So

The key here is to have a plan of action. First look at your highest values. Use this information to analyze your opportunities based on how many of your priorities are part of the overall job. Now look at what you especially liked about your current position. Use the first values exercise to help you here. Then look at the downside, or the reasons for wanting to move on. Using these as benchmarks, take some time at the library and see what you can learn about industries, careers and specific positions that fit your values and your skills and experience (either that which you have, or that you are willing to get). Once you've identified interesting areas to explore, go back to your priorities. Do these incorporate your highest values? Now's the time to take off the rose-colored glasses and determine what, if any, compromises will have to be made.

✳ *I sent Sara to the library with her benchmarks and assigned her many of the tasks you'll find in Chapter 6. When she returned she had a wealth of information.*

"I started with health care. It's a pretty big field. I looked at the dental side first. There are some surprising possibilities there, such as selling dental supplies. There are also dental hygienist schools and that opened up another whole avenue. A couple I found interesting were recruiting and public relations."

She also looked outside the dental field, particularly in the sales field. Pharmaceutical and hospital supplies didn't seem so far from dentistry.

Now it was time to go back to her priorities. At the top of the list were Security, Prestige, and Variety. She also wanted a position with growth potential and the challenge of something new and different, but in a relatively safe environment. She enjoyed interpersonal relations with people and wanted to establish those.

"I don't want to be stuck behind a desk, staring into a computer all day," she said.

Sales was far and away her first choice.

"I've always been self-motivated. My income's always been based on my own motivation. It wouldn't be any different in sales."

She outlined a career path as she saw it.

"My first step would be as a front line salesperson. From there I could move to sales director and finally to regional sales manager. Sales has the greatest potential for regaining my income."

I admired her self-confidence, but felt she needed to face the reality that a "commission only" position would compromise one of her highest values, Security.

"You're right, that's more risk than I'm willing to take," she admitted. She flung herself back in her chair, and looked up at the ceiling for a while.

"Not all sales positions are commission only," she concluded. "I would need to make that clear. I need the security of a regular paycheck, especially in a new field. It needn't be what I've been making, especially if I move to Seattle, but I'd have to count on it."

Sara left that day with a plan in her head. Her first choice was to look for a sales position with a dental supply house. If nothing came from that, she would look for a position with a dental hygienist school either in recruitment or public relations. If the dental field failed to produce for her, she would look into appropriate positions within the hospital supply and pharmaceutical fields.

All the way through our work together, one particular element stood out. Sara had a strong sense of her Professional Self. She saw herself as a highly skilled individual, she had a very positive sense of self, and felt quite confident that now that she had a game plan in hand, she could support herself and her children. She left looking forward to the challenge. ✳

The Company and the World It Operates In
Corporate Values

Another set of work values you should keep in mind might be labeled "Corporate Values." Sometimes this is reflected in the hierarchy of the company. Every job, especially at the management level, is shaped by the personal values, goals, and management style of the principal. Sometime during your working life you will probably be faced with a work situation that requires you to evaluate the organization and the employer, based on how well they mesh with your own values.

I interviewed once for a position with a highly visible elected official. After a few minutes of chit chat he asked how I had prepared for my interview.

"I checked you out," I said and told him how I had identified, contacted and interviewed people in the community who knew him.

He was surprised.

"If you and I are going to work closely in as visible a position as this," I told him, "I need to feel comfortable with what you stand for, what is important to you. I need to understand whether there are any conflicts regarding our individual stands on issues I know will be raised if I work here."

He leaned forward in his chair, looked at me over the tops of his half-glasses and asked, "Well, what did they say about me?"

"I'm here aren't I," I replied, and I got the job.

Sometimes corporate culture reflects more the corporate atmosphere you'll work in, but it is no less important. Jenny's experience illustrates this.

✱ *After she received her BA degree, and at her father's urging, she applied for a job at a bank. Her first assignment was as a teller. At this particular branch, the other tellers had little college experience. Dress tended towards short skirts and dramatic makeup. The cracking of chewing gum set her teeth on edge. Inept and unhappy behind the counter, she asked the manager to move her to accounting. This turned out to be no better. Jenny felt no closer to her co-workers who delighted in showing off pictures of their grandchildren. Finally the manager put her into a training program for loan officers. Here she found the social companionship she needed to feel comfortable with the job.*✱

Most organizations have a Code of Ethics or a Mission Statement that addresses the idea of corporate values. Amway and Mary Kay, for instance, besides being highly successful business concepts, incorporate specific value systems they expect to be honored. Patagonia Industries donates a percentage of its annual profits to organizations that strive to preserve the environment. Ben & Jerry's Ice Cream has decided their CEO will only earn eight times what its lowest paid worker makes. All of these are reflections of "corporate values." It is important, if you have strong feelings about certain issues, to research your potential employer with those feelings in mind. If they are in conflict, you must make some definite decisions regarding how much of your individual values and attitudes you are willing to compromise in order to fit comfortably into the organization.

Business organizations struggle with issues of social responsibility and corporate values all the time. There are no easy answers on how to solve major social ills facing the world today. Many do their best to prevent potential problems, but accidents do happen and attempts to resolve the problems are fraught with conflict. Others believe this is beyond the purview of business and ignore these issues altogether. In any case, you should never work for a company or a person where your basic values are in conflict. It is not fair to either of you.

All of life is a series of choices. Having a strong sense of your own values, you can use these to make those that will give you the greatest satisfaction, not only personally, but as a high "emotional salary."

✱ *Three months after I last met with Sara, I received a letter telling me she had settled into an apartment not far from her parents' home in*

Seattle and had accepted a position with a company that marketed prepaid dental plans. Last year's Christmas card included a note saying her year-end bonus put her just over the $35,000 mark, and she had made an offer on a house. ✳

Values Prioritization Exercise

Weigh each work value below on its importance to you and circle the number that most closely reflects your feeling (higher number = more important).

HIGH INCOME. Some minimum income (enough for survival) is essential for everyone. But beyond that, how important to you are the extras? People have different ideas about how much income is "high." Therefore, *high income* is not defined here as a specific amount. It means more than enough to live on. It means money to use as you wish after you have paid your basic living expenses. You can buy luxuries and travel first-class.

0   1   2   3   4   5   6   7   8

PRESTIGE. If people respect you, look up to you, listen to your opinions, or seek your help in community affairs, you are a person with *prestige*. Of course, *prestige* can be gained in several ways. But in present-day America, occupation is usually the key to *prestige*. Rightly or wrongly, we respect some occupations more than others.

0   1   2   3   4   5   6   7   8

INDEPENDENCE. Some occupations give you more freedom than others to make your own decisions, to work without supervision or direction from others. At one extreme might be talented freelance artists or writers who may work without supervision. At the other extreme might be military service or some big business organizations with chains of command which severely limit the decisions that each person can make.

0   1   2   3   4   5   6   7   8

HELPING OTHERS. Most people are willing to help others, and do it every day outside of their work. They put themselves out to do favors, make gifts, donate to charities, and so on. *This does not count here.* The question here is: Do you want *Helping others* to be a main part of your occupation? To what extent do you want to devote your life work directly to helping people improve their health, education or welfare?

0   1   2   3   4   5   6   7   8

SECURITY. In the most secure occupations, you will be free from fear of losing your job and income. You will have tenure— that is, you cannot be fired very easily. Employment will tend to remain high in spite of recessions, and there will be no seasonal ups and downs. Your income will usually remain stable and predictable; it will not vanish with hard times. Your occupation is not likely to be wiped out by automation or other technological changes.

0   1   2   3   4   5   6   7   8

VARIETY. Occupations with the greatest *variety* offer many different kinds of activities and problems, frequent changes in location, new people to meet. *Variety* is the opposite of routine, predictability, or repetition. If you value *variety* high, you probably like novelty and surprise, and enjoy facing new problems, events, places, and people.

0   1   2   3   4   5   6   7   8

LEADERSHIP. Do you want to guide others, tell them what to do, be responsible for their performance: People who weight *leadership* high usually want power to control events. They want to influence people to work together efficiently. If they are mature, they know that responsibility goes with *leadership*. They are willing to accept the blame when things go wrong, even though they were not at fault.

0   1   2   3   4   5   6   7   8

WORK IN YOUR MAIN FIELD OF INTEREST. Some people have only one main field of interest (science, engineering, business, helping others, writing, art or music); others are interested in two or more fields. Some insist that their occupation must be in one of their major fields of interest. Others are willing to work in a field that is less interesting; they feel they can satisfy their main interest in their spare time.

0   1   2   3   4   5   6   7   8

LEISURE. How important is the amount of time your occupation will allow you to spend away from work? Leisure may include short hours, long vacations, or the chance to choose your own time off. To give a high weight to *leisure* is like saying, "The satisfactions I get off the job are so important to me that work must not interfere with them."

0   1   2   3   4   5   6   7   8

CHALLENGE. Some people feel more satisfied when they expend great effort in solving problems at work. The presence of a problem demands their attention. Are you bored with easy work and stimulated with more difficult tasks? Would you prefer to work on assignments requiring real learning and effort?

0   1   2   3   4   5   6   7   8

INTERPERSONAL RELATIONS. Some occupations provide the opportunity to deal with people. Some people like to be a part of a team and to participate with others. Would working alone be undesirable to you? Do you enjoy the chance to meet people?

0	1	2	3	4	5	6	7	8

CREATIVITY. In some occupations you are encouraged to try out original solutions rather than rely on conventional tactics and established procedures. Are you proud of your ability to offer ideas in many situations? Do you have creative talents that you want to develop and use?

0	1	2	3	4	5	6	7	8

Scoring

For each section (1-12) enter your score under the column labeled "Initial Score." After the numbers have been entered, total the column. If the total exceeds a score of 48, go back to each value and adjust or eliminate original scores so that the total does not exceed 48. Enter those adjusted scores under the column labeled "Adjusted Score." In a sense you are ranking your values. This "Adjusted Score" should reflect those values about which you feel the strongest.

Values	Initial Score	Adjusted Score
(1) High Income	_____	_____
(2) Prestige	_____	_____
(3) Independence	_____	_____
(4) Helping Others	_____	_____

(5) Security   _____   _____

(6) Variety   _____   _____

(7) Leadership   _____   _____

(8) Interest Field   _____   _____

(9) Leisure   _____   _____

(10) Challenge   _____   _____

(11) Interpersonal Relations _____   _____

(12) Creativity   _____   _____

                 Total Weight _____   _____

1.   What are your three highest values?

2.   In what areas did you have to compromise?

"No person who is enthusiastic about his work has anything to fear from life." – Samuel Goldwyn

"Work is not primarily a thing one does to live, but the thing one lives to do. It is, or should be, the full expression of the worker's faculties, the thing in which he finds spiritual, mental and bodily satisfaction, and the medium in which he offers himself to God." – Dorothy L. Sayers

"The secret of life is to have a task, something you bring everything to, every minute of the day for your whole life. And the most important thing is – it must be something you cannot possibly do" – Henry Moore

5 Identifying Your Personality Style
Using it to create career satisfaction

"Throughout your life you'll have to deal with a number of different kinds of bosses, as well as peers and subordinates. An understanding of personality styles can help you improve your communications skills."

Maybe a job change is not warranted. Sometimes just knowing more about yourself and your coworkers will turn an impossible situation into a workable and rewarding one.

Similar personality styles have a tendency to get along well and can accomplish a great deal. But there can be too much of a good thing. Like-minded people tend to miss out on a variety of perspectives that lend flavor, dimension, and balance to the work place. The old adage that "opposites attract" is a good rule of thumb in order to insure maximum productivity. This is only true if we appreciate the unique contributions each person brings to the work place and realize that in an effective working unit each special talent contributes to the attitude, climate and productivity of the whole.

✱ *Natalie Weiss-Gordon was full of rage when she first came to see me.*

"Can you believe this?" She slammed a performance review down in front on me. "Never in my life have I been given a negative review. And he's pretty clear all right. He wants me out!"

What I observed before me was an attractive 32-year-old woman, wholesome looking, well put together in a conservative mode. Under-

neath this bravado she clearly felt embarrassed because of the situation that prompted her to come and see me.

As I reviewed the printed format with its hand written notes sprawled within each section, Natalie calmed herself down.

"It's more than just a poor review," she admitted in a quiet voice. "I care deeply about this job, and I believe I have done a good job. No one indicated any different. I am truly shocked."

She offered some background.

After graduating from the University of Illinois in Public Administration and working as an administrative analyst for the Department of Health and Human Services in Chicago for five years, she accompanied her husband to California where he took advantage of the then booming defense industry.

She immediately began looking at jobs with government agencies since that's what she knew, that's what she liked, and that's what she was comfortable with. Her past evaluations stood her in good stead, and within three months she landed an excellent position within the criminal justice system in San Diego helping to administer a Federal grant designed to teach parenting skills to women inmates who had a history of abusing their children.

"The grant is a result of the research done in the Minneapolis Domestic Violence Research Study," she told me, warming to her subject. "That study showed that battered women have a tendency to batter their children and those children have a tendency to marry into battering relationships. It creates a cyclical effect on families. The way we see it, children coming from dysfunctional families don't receive good parenting. This grant could have long-term ramifications by intercepting battering women while they are in jail and helping them develop appropriate parenting skills. If they feel good about one aspect of their lives, they can build on that and potentially rehabilitate themselves in other ways. This could benefit their children and their children's children. It is an important program, and I want to stay involved."

"How did you get to this point?" I asked, holding up the evaluation sheet.

"There are two phases to the grant," she began. "The first is a two-year start-up period for developing the program and enlisting support from various law enforcement agencies. The second part is a three-year grant working with the actual inmates. At the end of this first phase, if the program doesn't meet both the programmatic and the enrollment requirements, the rest of the money will go to two other pilot *programs, one in Philadelphia, the other in Maine, and that will be the end of it as far as this office is concerned."*

When Natalie was offered the position it was on a six-month probationary basis. This did not concern her, as she was confident in her ability.

She went to work for Ben Coburn, just three years out of a Master's program in Public Administration with emphasis in criminal justice and rehabilitation. The current grant was a continuation of the research for his master's thesis. Ben's major responsibility in this phase consisted chiefly of meeting with different law enforcement agencies, determining the needs of the female inmates through interviews, and gaining the support of the agencies through convincing them of the program's value.

"I've just finished my probationary period," Natalie explained. "I've been pleased with the progress of the project and pleased with my part in it. I was actually looking forward to my first performance review!" Her anger rose again.

"Ben says I lack self confidence, I'm not particularly verbal, and I need a great deal of supervision. He says I have potential to do the job, but he's not comfortable recommending me for a permanent position. He says he needs someone who is already capable, not someone with 'potential.' " She threw up her hands. "I cannot understand why, if Ben didn't like what I was doing, he never said anything to me. This is a real slap in the face."

"What did you do?"

"I refused to sign it. I went to the personnel office and asked to file a grievance charging poor supervision standards."

As part of the grievance process Natalie was required to discuss the evaluation with a career counselor, and that is what brought her here.

After extensive discussion of her reaction to the evaluation, I asked my bottom line question:

"What is it you want to happen as a result of this grievance?"

She was quite explicit. She wanted a new evaluation written with a clear understanding of what her strengths were and what benefits had accrued to the organization as a result of her being there, and she wanted some mediation and agreement between her and Ben as to her value and accomplishments. She chiefly felt that without her organizational skills, Ben's creativity would be lost.

The next step was to get Ben's side of the story. When he entered my office, I was impressed, just in terms of the difference in ap-

pearance and presence between the two. He was a contemporary Californian, 27 years old, blond and tan. I could see why he did so well in his public appearances. Once he got on stage, it was obvious that he knew his stuff and presented it very well. I could see where his personable boyish "one of the guys" charm would be welcomed by the law enforcement officials. His entire approach communicated his message: "We have a way to help you stop the revolving door of mothers, children, grandchildren going through your system. Together, let's make it happen."

I asked Ben to describe Natalie.

"She's a bean counter. She wants to make sure all our little ducks are in a row. She wants to make sure all the i's are dotted and t's are crossed all the time," he explained. "I see no point in doing any more of that than absolutely necessary. In most cases I believe the process takes care of itself."

It became obvious that one of the problems was a clash of personality styles, a clash between the way each interacted with the world around them, how they perceived their work, and how they perceived others. ✳

There is a natural human tendency to try to understand and relate to others as if their inner world were like our own. Unfortunately, this is not often the case. It's important to be able to understand the natural differences in the way human beings think and act. To maximize your effectiveness, you must first understand your own personality style and what that means in terms of strengths and weaknesses. An excellent tool for determining this is the Myers-Briggs Type Indicator (MBTI). This is the world's most popular measure of personality dispositions. Well over two million people have used it.

The Myers-Briggs Type Indicator traces its roots back to the theories of Swiss born psychiatrist C. G. Jung, who suggested that human behavior is not random but predictable, therefore classifiable. Jung went on to theorize that differences in behavior that seem so obvious to the naked eye, are a result of preferences related to the basic functions that our personalities perform throughout life. These tendencies have to do with how we approach life, work, and problem solving. These preferences emerge early in life and form the basis of our personalities, and become the core of our attractions to and aversions from people, tasks and events throughout our lives.

Ask any parent to describe their children as infants. They are able to clearly distinguish and describe the different personality styles of each child from the day they bring it home from the hospital.

After Jung's scholarly work appeared in English in 1923, Katherine Briggs, in collaboration with her daughter, Isabel Briggs-Myers spent the better part of the next decade trying to perfect a way to easily use Jung's theory in counseling situations. Thus the birth of the Myers-Briggs Type Indicator, the grandmother of a myriad group of personality analysis systems. It is frequently used in business and professional settings where people work in groups and need to deal constructively with differences.

For the career changer these indicators help you understand that much of your attraction toward tasks and responsibilities is the result of preferences developed early in life. They help you identify and understand these preferences, and you can use that information to identify the kinds of enterprises, positions, and corporate atmospheres that will provide your Professional Self with the most suitable climate for an enjoyable and meaningful work experience. I use this exercise twice in my career counseling process, once during the preliminary stages of personal exploration, and then again as we prepare for the interview. It gives my clients the "booster shot" of confidence through self awareness that ultimately leads to good interviews and from that to good job offers.

The indicators identify sixteen possible personality types, depending on how you measure along four specific bipolar dimensions:

- Extrovert/Introvert
- Sensing/Intuitive

- Thinking/Feeling
- Judging/Perceiving

The inventory helps you understand how you are likely to do your job, with what work environment you are most comfortable, how you like to take in information and make decisions, and where you focus your attention. It doesn't tell you that you've missed your calling as a spot welder. It helps you understand the kind of temperament you have, what combination of psychological and professional strengths you offer. For the most complete interpretation, take this inventory under the supervision of a trained career counselor. For a quick look at yourself and others around you, try the abbreviated exercise at the end of the chapter.

✴ *In each pair of traits, Natalie possessed the attributes of one, Ben of the other, a totally mismatched pair. Natalie turned out to be an ISTJ, which means she was Introverted, Sensing, Thinking and Judging. She was a classic Stabilizer in an organization, one of the people who likes to organize things, preserve tradition, emphasizing efficiency and attention to detail and a systematized approach to everything. She was an analytical manager of facts and details, dependable, decisive, painstaking, stable and conservative.*

Ben, on the other hand was an ENFP, an Extroverted, Intuitive, Feeling, Perceiving person. He exemplified the Catalyst, someone who is creative, imaginative, and individualistic in his approach to others. He was a warmly enthusiastic planner of change, individualistic; he pursued inspiration with impulsive energy and endeavored to understand and inspire others.

"Ben is always out in front making speeches, shaking hands, getting the law enforcement agencies to sign on to this program, yet nothing ever gets done back at the office because he is too busy doing those things," Natalie said. "We're going to be audited in another eight months. My concern is that if we don't get our facts and figures in order, we are going to lose funding for the rest of the grant. As Assistant Director I feel I have the responsibility for making sure this is happening. Ben says I'm too detail oriented and not terribly creative, that I

jump the gun in making decisions." She paused, then continued, "but somebody has to make the decisions."

Ben's view was predictably different. When I asked Ben to give me his honest opinion of Natalie and he sat back and thought about it for awhile. I could tell he was struggling with a lot of things. When he finally began, he spoke slowly, thoughtfully.

"You know I was part of the interview team that hired Natalie. We interviewed quite a few people. She wasn't my first choice, but I agreed to hire her because I thought she was good. Her evaluations from previous employers were stellar. She had great experience with the governmental process and although I thought she was a little too conservative and quiet, I believed she was going to be very good for the project and that's what disappoints me so much. We just don't seem to be on the same wave length. I know she wants this program to work. I want this program to work. But I just don't know how we can make it work together."

Both Natalie and Ben were competent individuals, and yet their work was becoming dysfunctional because they did not understand where the other was coming from. In every major aspect of how they looked at life their approaches were diametrically opposed. ✳

My World, As I See It
Personality Types

Extroverts tend to talk first and think later. They like being around groups of people both at work and socially, and crave approval. An estimated 75 percent of all adults are extroverts. Because they so greatly out number introverts, they often fail to realize that such a thing as introversion even exists.

And how differently Introverts act. They often develop a high level of concentration and can block out distractions. They also like people, but more on a one-to-one basis. They don't like having their privacy invaded. While often considered "good listeners," they can also perceived as aloof, shy, and sometimes even arrogant.

✻ *In the beginning Ben had taken Natalie with him as a partner to make presentations and help gather information. Although Natalie's presentations were adequate, it was quickly apparent to Ben that it was not easy or natural for her to speak in front of a group. He was disappointed that she was unable to reach the audiences as well as he did. As time went on he found himself leaving her behind more and more frequently, and he interpreted this as failure on her part. On the other hand, when he left her at the office, it only caused more trouble.*

"When she's there she wants to run everything," he complained. "She is the Assistant Director. She's constantly reworking budgets and doing things I am responsible for."

Ben resented Natalie deciding without consulting him first. Natalie was appalled at Ben's not making decisions at all. Ben, on the other hand, had expected his assistant to help with the presentations. As an Extrovert, he didn't see this as any problem. He derived his energy from being around a lot of people, and he assumed everyone else did, too. He was a kind of cheerleader, and wanted her to be as excited about making presentations as he was and couldn't understand her discomfort. ✻

In determining how we choose to gather data, the differences between the Sensing and Intuitive aspects were equally as wide. Sensors more often choose occupations where they can achieve practical results with tangible things. Intuitives generally prefer to give general answers to questions and are annoyed when people push them for detail. Their concentration tends to be scattered and their friends often accuse them of being absent minded. One the other hand, Sensors have been accused of nit-picking.

✻ *I told Ben that one of Natalie's primary concerns was there had not been enough attention to detail regarding the audit. Ben very matter-of-factly said he had set aside the last month of the first phase to work on the audit and that he didn't want to look at much of it until then.*

Intuitives are more frequently found among psychotherapists, strategic planners, philosophy professors and lawyers – those occupations where there are no right or wrong answers. If you are a Sensor and your supervisor is more on the Intuitive side, he may misinterpret your asking a lot of detail questions before beginning an assignment as lack of confidence or inability to perform the job functions. All the while you may see his lack of clear direction as poor or weak leadership. It may be misinterpreted on your part as unprofessional management style. This is an easy trap to fall into if you are an Intuitive, as 70 percent of the U. S. population are Sensors.

The same kinds of conflicts are apt to present themselves in how Thinkers and Feelers typically make decisions in their lives. Thinkers are likely to assume that logic applies to everyone, and that those who don't operate this way are simply using logic poorly. They tend to behave independently within their own internal mechanisms to come up with enough pros and cons to be comfortable making decisions. They've been accused of being cold and uncaring.

Feelers don't like conflict and tend to be accommodating. They make decisions using a very personalized, subjective, values-driven process. They tend to be ruled by compassion rather than logic. Thinkers often consider them wishy-washy. If you are the only Feeler in a group of Thinkers you will undoubtedly feel persecuted and put upon at work. You will not understand their matter of fact way of doing business and be somewhat alarmed by what you observe as their callous way of making decisions.

Men have traditionally been thought of as Thinkers and women as Feelers. However, this is not as lopsided as once presumed. Recent surveys have shown that about 40 percent of men are Feelers, and about 40 percent of women are Thinkers.

The last two sets of preferences take a look at how people tend to orient their lives.

✳ *Ben was a Perceiver. It was very difficult for him to make decisions because he was an information gatherer. Every time he reached a point where he had to make a critical judgment, as far as Natalie saw it, he went out in the field to get more information. This caused one of the major bones of contention between the two.* ✳

As you can see, this aspect of their personalities reflected the way they preferred to interact with the world and the way they preferred to receive stimulation and energy.

✳ *Natalie was a Judger. She was decisive, firm, and sure. She set goals and stuck to them. Decisions came easy to her, but, according to Ben, she made decisions without enough information. Like most Judgers, Natalie wanted to close the books and get on to the next project. When a project does not yet have closure, Judgers often leave it behind and go on to new tasks and don't look back.* ✳

Judgers have a tendency to be regimented and don't like surprises. They are sometimes accused of being angry when they're only stating an opinion.

Perceivers often believe they do not make good decisions because of a sense of foreboding that overcomes them once they have committed themselves. They begin to think about the possibilities they have eliminated, the options that are no longer available, and spend a lot of time contemplating the "what if's." Their forte is information and opinion gathering, but when it comes down to deciding they become very uncomfortable and tend to shy away, opting to gather more information.

Decision making will never be easy for Perceivers. It helps, however, if they can understand that their discomfort stems from the process of decision making, not necessarily from making poor decisions. This understanding will enable them to develop coping strategies which can make the process less stressful and can increase their effectiveness as decision makers. It is important to get them to understand they can and will make good judgments but at the same time acknowledge that there will always be a certain amount of discomfort when they do.

These last two characteristics are the most evenly divided. In the general population, fifty-five percent of people have a judging preference while forty-five percent are Perceivers.

Some combinations of these eight characteristics are found more frequently among certain occupations. For instance in a recent study of lawyers, more than half are represented by just four of the possible sixteen types, and three of those four included the Thinker-Judger combination. The Sensor-Feeler combination is often found among pharmacists. Some common characteristics of the various personality styles will be found at the end of the chapter.

�號 *Meanwhile Natalie and Ben continued to work together at the office under an agreement that they not discuss their differences. I wanted them to think about the differences and their strengths and weaknesses independently, without input from the other or from their coworkers. I suggested that Ben continue his speaking engagements and, at least for now, he allow Natalie to review the budgets in preparation for the audit, giving her some relief from her anxiety over not being prepared.*

After reviewing the results of the MBTI, I recommended we meet with a representative of the personnel department. Prior to the meeting I sat down with Ben and Natalie independently and thoroughly discussed their individual personality styles, their competencies and limitations, and what each style brought to the organization.

The ultimate goal of their working together was to preserve, modify, and improve the working relationship so as to ensure the adequate functioning of the grant. It was very similar to couples counseling in that individuals within the couple need to understand if the relationship is to continue, there needs to be compromise and understanding on both parts. Neither is wrong, neither is right. They need to understand what their differences are, come to some kind of mutual accord in terms of how each is going to accept and respect those differences and work with them. They need to develop a working relationship that plays on the strengths of each, and mitigates the weaknesses.

Ben and Natalie represent an extreme but not uncommon case. They also had the benefit of a personnel department that referred them to a trained career counselor. As you look at your own situation, you may find yourself on your own. ✻

Knowledge is Power
Working Effectively with Diversity

To understand the dynamics in your own work situation, see how well the results of the exercise at the end of the chapter fits the way you approach life, work and problem solving.

Next identify the characteristics of the person or persons at work who are contributing to your discomfort. See if these characteristics fit a personality style in conflict with yours. Ask yourself,

- "How do I feel about people who operate with this style?"
- "How do I usually relate with these people?"
- "What can I do to deal more effectively with this style?"

Start by identifying and appreciating the strengths of this style. Then look at the weaknesses and see what can be done to minimize your conflict. Do your best to work out your differences. It will help you determine whether it is feasible to remain in your present situation. You can decide if you want to accommodate the other person. You can ask to be accommodated. You might want to seek the aid of a career counselor to help you clarify the issues you are dealing with and work out a solution.

The above is a good exercise to practice with the variety of personality styles you come in contact with on a daily basis. This can have far reaching effects. Throughout your life you'll have to deal with a number of different kinds of bosses, as well as peers and subordinates. An understanding of personality styles can help you improve your communications skills especially where you or someone else has one of the less frequent characteristics. For instance, you can adapt your own style of communication to be more like that of the individual you're trying to influence. It can also help you in dealing with clients, or marketing your services to a prospective client. You'll be able to step back, understand how the person's type preferences appear to differ from your own, and adjust your communication in a way they can most easily accept. Your overall success will increase in proportion to how well you work with each of these situations. You'll make yourself, as well as well as everyone else look good.

✱ *I met with Ben and Natalie again independently before the meeting, and with their consent, discussed the other's results and how that affected their relationship and their ability to work with each other. They began to understand that there were no pathological or psychological malfunctions on the part of either.*

Prior to the meeting I also asked them to recommend to me how they would restructure their work responsibilities in order to highlight their own strengths and to minimize their weaknesses. I asked them to come up with four recommendations and submit them to me in writing. I reviewed them, incorporated my own recommendations and then presented the package to them and the personnel officer all at once. By this time, Natalie and Ben had had an opportunity to understand their differences and were beginning to feel less hostile towards each other.

"First let me suggest the position of Assistant Director be rewritten and that the Assistant Director assume primary responsibility for record keeping and report writing for the purpose of grant reporting and auditing. As Director, Ben, you will still be able to review and approve the final draft."

This left Ben's power intact, but made the process easier for them both and gave Natalie something solid to bite into.

"I also feel the Assistant Director should be able to develop the necessary systems and support to provide the appropriate documentation for the grant reporting."

Having this in writing gave Natalie the permission she needed to develop these without having to bug Ben with detail questions. In effect, it allowed the process to take care of itself via Natalie.

"I think everyone will be more comfortable if you remove Natalie's responsibility for public presentations from the job description."

I suggested that once a week they meet, over a two-hour lunch, to discuss both long and short term assignments. This provided structure for Ben in a manner he could accept because of the informality of lunch. Natalie would give Ben a list of things that needed to be accomplished by the end of the month. She presented goals rather than struc-

*ture. However he chose to accomplish those goals was then his deci-
sion.*

*These meetings gave Natalie the structure she needed. She knew
with certainty that on Friday afternoons, for two hours she had Ben's
undivided attention. As I worked with Natalie and Ben over the next
four months, they began to develop a remarkable sense of respect for
what each of them brought to the project. And while they never saw
eye to eye on everything, Ben became much more confident in Natalie's
ability to handle matters; Natalie became much less critical of Ben's
style and much more appreciative of his flamboyance and creativity.
They truly became working partners as each strove to become supportive of the other, ensuring that both shone like the stars they were.*

*As a result Ben rewrote the evaluation, and Natalie dropped her
complaint about his management style. The project flourished under
this new working relationship.* ✻

If you decide a career change is necessary, this knowledge
of personality style will be an invaluable guide in choosing your
next employer. For instance, by paying attention to personality
styles you will have an early warning system as to how your new
boss is likely to operate. You can then tailor your interview responses in the most effective terms, giving the most appropriate
information for that style. On the other hand, you may be able
to decide quickly, based on the style you see, that this would not
be a happy marriage and move on.

Personal Style Inventory

The following items are arranged in pairs (a and b), and each member of the pair represents a preference you may or may not hold. Rate your preference for each item by giving it a score of 0 to 5 (0 represents the negative end of the scale, 5 the positive). The scores for a and b must add up to 5 (0 and 5, 1 and 4, etc.) A score of 0 and 5 could mean that you feel really negative about it or that you strongly prefer the other.

I prefer:

1a. _____ making decisions after finding out what others think.
1b. _____ making decisions without consulting others.

2a. _____ being called imaginative or intuitive.
2b. _____ being called factual and accurate.

3a. _____ making decisions about people in organizations based on available data and systematic analysis of situations.
3b. _____ making decisions about people in organizations based on empathy, feelings and understanding of their needs and values.

4a. _____ allowing commitments to occur if others want to make them.
4b. _____ pushing for definite commitments to ensure that they are made.

5a. _____ quiet, thoughtful time alone.
5b. _____ active, energetic time with people.

6a. _____ using methods I know well that are effective to get the job done.

6b. _____ trying to think of new methods of doing tasks when confronted with them.

7a. _____ drawing conclusions based on unemotional logic and careful step-by-step analysis.
7b. _____ drawing conclusions based on what I feel and believe about life and people from past experiences.

8a. _____ avoiding making deadlines.
8b. _____ setting a schedule and sticking to it.

9a. _____ talking awhile and then thinking to myself about the subject.
9b. _____ talking freely for an extended period and thinking to myself at a later time.

10a. _____ thinking about possibilities.
10b. _____ dealing with actualities.

11a. _____ being thought of as a thinking person.
11b. _____ being thought of as a feeling person.

12a. _____ considering every possible angle for a long time before and after making a decision.
12b. _____ getting the information I need, considering it for a while, and then making a fairly quick, firm decision.

13a. _____ inner thoughts and feelings others cannot see.
13b. _____ activities and occurrences in which others join.

14a. _____ the abstract or theoretical.
14b. _____ the concrete or real.

15a. _____ helping others explore their feelings.
15b. _____ helping others make logical decisions.

16a. _____ change and keeping options open.
16b. _____ predictability and knowing in advance.

17a. _____ communicating little of my inner thinking and feelings.
17b. _____ communicating freely my inner thinking and feelings.

18a. _____ possible views of the whole.
18b. _____ the factual details available.

19a. _____ using common sense and conviction to make decisions.
19b. _____ using data, analysis, and reason to make decisions.

20a. _____ planning ahead based on projections.
20b. _____ planning as necessities arise, just before carrying out the plans.

21a. _____ meeting new people.
21b. _____ being alone or with one person I know well.

22a. _____ ideas.
22b. _____ facts.

23a. _____ convictions.
23b. _____ verifiable conclusions.

24a. _____ keeping appointments and notes about commitments in notebooks or in appointment books as much as possible.
24b. _____ using appointment books and notebooks as minimally as possible (although I may use them).

25a. _____ discussing a new, unconsidered issue at length in a group.

25b. _____ puzzling out issues in my mind, then sharing the results with another person.

26a. _____ carrying out carefully laid, detailed plans with precision.

26b. _____ designing plans and structures without necessarily carrying them out.

27a. _____ logical people.

27b. _____ feeling people.

28a. _____ being free to do things on the spur of the moment.

28b. _____ knowing well in advance what I am expected to do.

29a. _____ being the center of attention.

29b. _____ being reserved.

30a. _____ imagining the nonexistent.

30b. _____ examining details of the actual.

31a. _____ experiencing emotional situations, discussions, movies.

31b. _____ using my ability to analyze situations.

32a. _____ starting meetings at a prearranged time.

32b. _____ starting meetings when all are comfortable or ready.

Personal Style Inventory Scoring Sheet

Instructions: Transfer your scores for each item of each pair to the appropriate blanks. Be careful to check the a and b letters to be sure you are recording scores in the right blank spaces. Then total the scores for each dimension.

DIMENSION		DIMENSION	
I	E	N	S
Item	Item	Item	Item
1b. _____	1a. _____	2a. _____	2b. _____
5a. _____	5b. _____	6b. _____	6a. _____
9a. _____	9b. _____	10a. _____	10b. _____
13a. _____	13b. _____	14a. _____	14b. _____
17a. _____	17b. _____	18a. _____	18b. _____
21b. _____	21a. _____	22a. _____	22b. _____
25b. _____	25a. _____	26b. _____	26a. _____
29b. _____	29a. _____	30a. _____	30b. _____

TOTAL

I _____   E _____   N _____   S _____

DIMENSION		DIMENSION	
T	F	P	J
Item	Item	Item	Item
3a. _____	3b. _____	4a. _____	4b. _____
7a. _____	7b. _____	8a. _____	8b. _____
11a. _____	11b. _____	12a. _____	12b. _____
15a. _____	15b. _____	16a. _____	16b. _____
19b. _____	19a. _____	20b. _____	20a. _____
23b. _____	23a. _____	24b. _____	24a. _____

27a. _____   27b. _____   28a. _____   28b. _____
31b. _____   31a. _____   32b. _____   32a. _____

TOTAL
T _____   F _____   P _____   J _____

Personality Styles in the Workplace

Introverts

Like quiet for concentration.

Tend to be careful with details, dislike sweeping statements.

Have trouble remembering names and facts.

Tend not to mind working on one project for a long time without interruption.

Are interested in the idea behind their job.

Dislike telephone intrusions and interruptions.

Like to think a lot before they act, sometimes without acting.

Work contentedly alone.

Have some problems communicating.

Extroverts

Like variety and action.

Tend to be faster, dislike complicated procedures.

Are often good at greeting people.

Are often impatient with long, slow jobs.

Are interested in the results of their job, in getting it done, and in how other people do it.

Often do not mind the interruption of answering the telephone.

Often act quickly, sometimes without thinking.

Like to have people around.

Usually communicate freely.

Sensing Types

Dislike new problems unless there are standard ways to solve them.

Like an established way of doing things.

Enjoy using skills already learned more than learning new ones.

Work more steadily, with a realistic idea of how long it will take.

Usually reach a conclusion step by step.

Are patient with routine details.

Are impatient when details get complicated.

Are more often inspired, and rarely trust the inspiration when they are.

Seldom make errors of fact.

Tend to be good at precise work.

Intuitive Types

Like solving new problems.

Dislike doing the same thing repeatedly.

Enjoy learning a new skill more than using it.

Work in bursts of energy powered by enthusiasm, with slack periods in between.

Reach a conclusion quickly.

Are impatient with routine details.

Are patient with complicated situations.

Follow their inspirations, good or bad.

Frequently make errors of fact.

Dislike taking time for precision.

Thinking Types

Do not show emotion readily and are often uncomfortable dealing with people's feelings.

May hurt people's feelings without knowing it.

Like analysis and putting things into logical order. Can get along without harmony.

Tend to decide impersonally, sometimes paying insufficient attention to people's wishes.

Need to be treated fairly.

Are able to reprimand people or fire them when necessary.

Are more analytically oriented – respond more easily to people's thoughts.

Tend to be firm-minded.

Feeling Types

Tend to be very aware of other people and their feelings.

Enjoy pleasing people, even in unimportant things.

Like harmony. Efficiency may be badly disturbed by office feuds.

Often let decisions be influenced by their own or other people's personal likes and wishes.

Need occasional praise.

Dislike telling people unpleasant things.

Are more people-oriented–respond more easily to people's values.

Tend to be sympathetic.

Judging Types

Work best when they can plan their work and follow the plan.

Like to get things settled and finished.

May decide things too quickly.

May dislike to interrupt the project they are on for a more urgent one.

May not notice new things that need to be done.

Want only the essentials needed to begin their work.

Tend to be satisfied once they reach a judgment on a thing, situation, or person.

Perceptive Types

Adapt well to changing situations.

Do not mind leaving things open for alterations.

May have trouble making decisions.

May start too many projects and have difficulty in finishing them.

May postpone unpleasant jobs.

Want to know all about a new job.

Tend to be curious and welcome new light on a thing, situation, or person.

Getting Job Market Research to Pay Off

- **Learn to use resources already available in your community.**

- **Frame your career search in the context of a world economy.**

- **Learn specific techniques for exploring industries and positions.**

- **Experience the powerful feeling of control and choice.**

6 Researching Your Options
Identifying and targeting the markets

> *"Many career changers, who wouldn't think of buying a car or a VCR without doing exhaustive research, know almost nothing about the company they are pursuing."*

Most people start their job search by looking for positions. They immediately begin searching the want ads for a job. They see little opportunity and discouragement immediately sets in. Searching for positions should be fourth on your list as you begin to research the job market. Your first need is to gain perspective. What is happening in the global economy that is going to affect my job here in my hometown? How is this going to matter in terms of job security or the kinds of work I want to do? What is happening nationally? For that matter, what is happening in my own community? What industries are ebbing or flowing? In the flourishing industries, which companies will be the leaders?

* *Barbara Miller bounded into my office, shook my hand, plopped herself into the chair and immediately tucked one foot under the casual jeans she was wearing.*

"I'm twenty-nine years old, and I need some direction in my life," she began. *"I've done a lot of things so far. I've supported myself since I left high school. I've traveled through most of the U. S. I've shod horses in Montana, cooked on a freighter on the Mississippi, and strung racquets at a country club in Atlanta. I went back to school and discovered I had two passions: biology and art. I graduated last spring with a double major."*

"And now you need a job."

"Not just any job. I'm older now, I'll be thirty in the spring. I want to settle down. I want something stable. Something for the long haul."
She straighten her leg from under her and leaned forward. "I'm lean and mean and ready for somebody to reap the benefits of not only my education, but of my state of mind. And I don't know how to go about finding that." ✳

Many career changers, who wouldn't think of buying a car or a VCR without doing exhaustive research, know almost nothing about the company they are pursuing, who runs it, what the prospects are for its immediate future, or for its industry as a whole. To be successful, it is imperative you take a look at the overall job market and get an idea of where you fit in. It's about as much fun as looking for a car, but the rewards are just as tangible. This research usually transcends all aspects of your career search and should begin the moment you decide you want make a change.

But what do you look for and how do you know when you have found it? Once you have found it, how do you use it?

- By looking at global and national issues you establish a context for your search.
- You'll use that knowledge to identify growing industries.
- Then look for growing industries that mesh with your interests.
- From these you'll explore the variety of positions available in those industries.
- Finally, you'll investigate specific employers who have job openings that interest you.

Start with some very general resources. Read the business section of your daily newspaper and weekly magazines like *Time* and *U.S. News & World Report*. Get acquainted with professional journals and business and industry guides. See what your library has to offer.

Basically you want to train your mind to **recognize** and **accept information** about careers and economic trends **that is readily available as part of your daily life**. You need to train yourself to become a *career consumer*. Think of yourself as a detective as you search out these trends. You need to develop a "third eye," a career focus if you will, with which to view the world. As you begin to filter information through this third eye, everything you read will be career oriented, you'll see opportunities everywhere. But until it becomes part of your regular repertoire, the information is just going to bounce right off you as if it hit a Teflon shield. Aim for the Velcro effect, where the information sticks.

As you become more facile at conducting employer research and organizing your materials it will become obvious the kinds of information you will need and what is the quickest and easiest way to access that information. Look at this part of your job search as developing a new skill that will improve your problem solving techniques. Think of yourself as an investigator, hot on the trail of "The Hidden Job Market." Sure you'll run into some red herrings, and some leads will be dead ends, but the clues will begin to build on one another, and in the end, you'll unravel it all and come to a successful conclusion.

As you begin your research, you need to develop a system for keeping information straight. Notes, comments and thoughts regarding the trends, industries, companies and positions you will be learning about should be cataloged and organized in a way that will help you evaluate how they fit your current needs.

Keep a journal on the information you read, and make yourself a two-week deadline for your first intensive foray into career research. Deadlines are important when people are beginning the general part of a job search as it makes them accountable and heads off procrastination. At this point the initial information might not seem relevant. As you develop a framework for it, you will find little hooks on which to hang each bit of information. As you progress, the information you derived from this preliminary investigation will become more important and valuable to you.

What in the World is Going On?
Global Issues

It should come as no surprise that we live in a global economy. Car parts are manufactured all over the world and gathered in one place for assembly. To assume that international events don't have an effect on local economies is folly. Regularly reading news magazines will give you significant information on the kinds of global happenings that will affect you in the marketplace. For instance, as companies struggle to control domestic labor costs, more positions become available overseas. Through international trade agreements like GATT and NAFTA, our trading borders have exploded. The break up of the communist bloc alone opened up thirty percent of the world to new economic opportunities. It also precipitated the downsizing of the Defense Department which dramatically affected the aerospace industry. China is the fastest growing economy in today's world. What does that mean to the rest of us?

Two books I highly recommend to start you off are *Megatrends 2000* by John Naisbitt and Patricia Aburdene, and *The Global Paradox*, by John Naisbitt. These books are a "must read" for all my clients. They not only identify major global trends of the '90s, but the discussion, based on research by these two authors, contains a great deal of useful economic information you'll call upon as you move through the process.

The goal here is to relate economic and global trends and issues to the information you have gathered about your Professional Self. It's important to look at this information at the very beginning of a job search as it helps you create an attitude that you have choices, and this gives you power.

✳ *I could see Barbara was not enthusiastic about all that reading.*

"I'm not asking you to read everything from cover to cover," I assured her. *"Sample everything and take only the information you feel is valuable or interesting. Read the books in your leisure time. Take them to the beach. Leave yourself time to assimilate and process what they have to offer."*

Barbara arrived in my office two weeks later in a state of confusion.

"I am totally saturated with all the stuff I've soaked up. I feel like a sponge," she admitted as she again flung herself into the chair.

"Which book made the biggest impression on you?" I asked.

"Far and away it was Megatrends 2000. Two of the major directions they talk about are the renaissance of the arts and the resurgence of the physical sciences such as biology. Here, all of a sudden, I find a national best seller confirming both my major fields!"

This was what I was hoping for: That out of these there would be one or two items that stood out as having information specifically useful to her. ✳

What's Good in the USA is Good for Me
National Trends

Now take a look at what's going on here at home. National politics and their swings have a significant affect on economic sectors. Republican agendas tend to be more internationally based, defense aligned, more economically or business oriented. Democratic agendas tend to focus on domestic, social and education issues. Whoever is in the driver's seat will affect the kinds of economies that are going to matter on the job front. In any given year, budgets decided on in Washington, D.C. profoundly affect the kinds of jobs that are out there. If for instance, you are looking for a research grant from the National Endowment of the Arts, you'd have a better chance at winning it under a Democratic Congress. If you were looking for a grant from the National Security Council, you'll have better luck under a Republican regime.

Current demographics are equally important. Take the baby boomers, for example.

According to an Associated Press analysis of 1990 census data, baby boomers (those born between 1946 and 1964) now make up nearly one-third of the U. S. population. As they age, the marketplace is looking for what they will want. As a group they have created another baby boom, although family size is generally smaller than a generation ago. They are in their prime earning years. They are also in their prime spending years, as they buy homes and prepare for college costs. New spending patterns indicate, for instance, that family restaurants are becoming more popular. Health and safety issues are growing concerns.

In the next ten years, the 45-to-54 age group will increase 44 percent, according to the Census Bureau. These will be predominately white, driving the demand for medical and leisure services, in addition to security services, restaurants and financial and retirement planning. The growth in the younger generation will be increasingly non-white with Hispanics growing at the fastest rate. What will be their needs?

In recessions, when massive layoffs become the news of the day, some industries prosper, out-placement counseling for instance. Discount retail stores, low cost leisure activities such as bowling and pool, video shops and fast food eateries tend to do well. One entrepreneurial hair salon profited from the most recent recession by positioning itself as a moderately priced full service salon, and attracted the newly cost conscious who still wanted maximum service.

✳ *To help her understand the possibilities, I asked Barbara to look for job and career fairs that focused on professional positions. These fairs are often listed in your local paper in the classified section under "employment," or you might find them advertised at career centers, your local state employment center, the Small Business Administration or the chamber of commerce.*

Barbara came racing back to my office after seeing a hundred or so employers at one job fair in the Los Angeles Coliseum. She was both excited and frustrated.

"I think I could work for every one of them, and be happy. How can I narrow down what I am looking for in an organization and how can I become more comfortable with my choices? I don't want to start jumping around again. I want to settle down, join a company where I make a difference, and where I can move up the ladder. I need to narrow down my choices and make a good decision." ✳

Industry-wise, What's Hot? What's Not?
Industry Trends

Look through the information on various industries, companies and career possibilities you've collected so far and identify those that will flourish, those that will languish. Think of these in the broad sense: technology, finance, education, engineering, consumer products, leisure, health and fitness. My personal opinion is that civil engineering will be a booming field in the near future, because of the state of disrepair of the infrastructure nationwide. Good news for civil and structural engineers, as well as construction workers and the industries that support these professions.

Evaluate the general climate of the healthy industries that mesh with your interests, and identify those factors relevant to their success at this time. To do this you need to get acquainted with your local librarian. You might be surprised at how friendly research librarians are. Rather than esoteric recluses, these people have been hired specifically to help people find whatever information they need. This can be anything from the Blue Book price of a used car to computer searches for stock market bargains. No question is too far out, or too simple, for them.

To begin with, they probably will direct you to the business and financial sections. They'll acquaint you with business and trade directories, periodical indexes, and abstracts and tell you what you can expect to find in them. They'll tell you about their "vertical files," that section of the library containing pamphlets and news clippings, which is probably your best bet for local information. They will also steer you towards any specialized business collections in other libraries in your area, such as at a university. These libraries are usually open to you as well, even if you don't have a card, as long as you use the material while you are there. Many of these have evening and weekend hours.

A good place to start, in any library, is with the *Reader's Guide to Periodical Literature*. In many libraries the periodical index now runs on a computer, which is easier and faster. Look up general topics like "jobs." Many major magazines run general surveys on "Where the hot jobs are." Or look under specific industries. You will even find articles about specific companies.

Another good source for this kind of information is the *U. S. Industrial Outlook*, prepared by the U. S. Department of Labor. It gives key data on over 350 different industries, such as general overviews, employment statistics, foreign competition, impact from technology, growth forecasts, career trends, and production and sales statistics. Each chapter gives a summary of the past year's performance, and positive and negative aspects that will affect the future. Standard and Poor's publishes similar material and includes financial comparisons of leading companies in each of the 25 major industries it profiles.

✳ *When Barbara returned for our next meeting, she had the information she needed to narrow down her fields and to make some informed choices. She had investigated several of the areas she had been excited about at the trade show. She checked the library's periodical guide for pertinent articles, and leafed through the Occupational Outlook Handbook, and New Emerging Careers: Today, Tomorrow and in the 21st Century, by S. Norman Feingold and Norma Reno Miller. She separated the expanding areas from the contracting ones. She also came away with names of several successful companies in each expanding area. This investigation would also help her avoid interviews with companies in economic difficulty, and not waste valuable time exploring positions for which she was not qualified.* ✳

Now write down what you imagine to be the ideal size, location, client mix, work environment, and project approach for your present career goals. Next look for firms that closely fit that description. A common assumption is that you won't know many of these until you're hired. True, there is a lot you will have to assume or trust your judgment on, but there are resources that can provide you with some insight as to how an organization feels about its employees and attitudes within the organization that may influence you one way or another.

Check out *The American Almanac of Jobs and Salaries,* particularly if you are a bit fuzzy about the industries you are interested in and are having a difficult time pinpointing the kinds of positions you might want to look at. This book gives you an opportunity to survey a variety of jobs in terms of specific tasks, salaries, etc. The book contains close to 15,000 job descriptions, everything from rodeo clown to investment banker and a considerable variety of government positions. It is the most comprehensive guide in terms of job descriptions and what you can expect as starting salaries.

Another book I recommend is *The Best Companies for Women.* This book looks at benefits, which is particularly important if you're looking forward to marriage and a family or are already in that situation. You might also want to check *Companies That Care,* by Hal Morgan & Kerry Tucker. Some of these books are updated regularly, and there are new ones out each year, so be sure to look over the entire career book section at your library.

✳ *After reading through half of New Emerging Careers: Today, Tomorrow and in the 21st Century, Barbara began to see the validity of scrutinizing individual companies in terms of health and safety factors, insurance benefits, retirement benefits, stock options, early retirement packages, maternity leave, all of the issues she felt were going to be important to her as a working professional.*

Barbara had a lot of interests and to help her narrow these down, she worked through the Values Exercise (Chapter 4). She found her top priorities centered on creativity, independence and working within her two disciplines. We now began to establish some criteria, including an opportunity to grow and an opportunity for artistic expression. Barbara also felt a tremendous pull towards the sciences as well as art and wasn't quite sure which direction she favored. As we began to talk more about the kinds of organizations she wanted to work for, she focused first on artistic areas. If there was any way she could combine her two interests, that would just be frosting on the cake. ✳

What I Can Do For You
Researching Specific Positions

Now your personal desires and research begin to pay off. Your chances of hitting the bull's eye are far greater when you have a target than when you don't. Positions will jump out at you because you know what you have to market.

To expand your possibilities, look at career books in your particular area. VGA, for instance, publishes a whole series of *Opportunities in...* and *Careers in...* books. If you don't find material in your career field, ask the librarian if it is available from another library through the inter-library loan program.

Ask to see *Standard Directory of Advertisers,* published by Standard Rate and Data Service, Inc. This guide indexes, by business category, all trade publications that accept paid advertising. Suppose you're interested in the travel industry, but aren't aware of any job possibilities other than flight attendant or travel agent, and neither appeals to you. In this guide you'll find listings for several travel-related magazines, each directed to a different group of people in the travel business. You can get back issues of these magazines and explore the different kinds of jobs available in each area.

Two invaluable resources are *The Encyclopedia of Associations and Organizations* and *The American Trade and Professional Associations Directory.* These list thousands of organizations whose primary goals are to promote their particular field, and they are excellent sources of information. You can call the associations in your field and ask if there are local chapters and contact numbers. Find out if they have meetings. Ask for businesses that are affiliated with the organization. Ask about current trends.

Belonging to a professional organization is one of the best ways to get up-to-date literature and information on openings and trends in your field. I refer clients to these encyclopedias almost daily and almost daily they tell me about the valuable information they received when they wrote and asked for directories.

✱ *"I'm getting a reputation for carrying the world's heaviest beach bag," Barbara laughed when we next met. "I've also found a lovely little espresso bar that serves great cappuccino and doesn't mind my hogging a table for hours. Every now an then someone even comes up and asks to look at some of the books."*

For her homework I suggested she skim through High Tech Jobs for Non Tech Graduates, because I felt Barbara's science background ws still worthy of consideration and exploration. Other resources I suggested, such as Professionals' Job Finder, by Daniel Lauber, and A Directory of Information Resources in the U.S, Physical Sciences, Engineering, were more closely related to her specific interests.

I began to sense that the beach scene and cappuccino were wearing thin. "All I'm doing is looking at books, looking at books. I'm finding out more information, but I'm not sure where it's leading," Barbara grumbled.

"I think this will bring it into focus," I explained to her. "Start ranking the kinds of things you want in an organization and potential positions you might be interested in."

The list she returned to me was heavily weighted towards museums: art museums, museums of natural history, museums of space and technology, those kinds of things. Also included were medical publishers. I asked how she arrived at her list.

"I located most of it in A Directory of Information Resources in the U. S. Here I found places where I can combine my artistic talent with science," she replied. "For instance, I'd never thought about medical illustration."

Building on this, I suggested as her next task she look at what it takes to be a medical illustrator.

The library was again the initial source for her information. By now she and the research librarian had become fast friends and he helped her locate whatever was available. At our next meeting, Barbara's enthusiasm was still evident, but more focused, the information she had uncovered now creating its own momentum. She had already contacted a medical illustrator's organization and gone to one of its meetings.

"It was wonderful," she said, her animation bubbling up again. "I found out about places where I could get additional training and certification. I also learned that one of the key components to being a good medical illustrator is having a fine arts background, particularly working with the human form."

I could see she was really excited about this.

"When I was in school, I always entered work in the art shows. I did pretty well, too. Even Best of Show in a couple of them, and they were juried shows, too. And how about this? My best award was for a series of pen and ink drawings of the human figure!" She could hardly sit still. She also felt this was an excellent way for her to use her biology background. Her excitement carried her to the medical library at several of the local hospitals and the medical school at a nearby university.

"I've spent hours pouring over those books looking at the illustrations. I believe I've had found my niche."

I asked her, "Why?"

"Because my heart starts beating faster when I look at this work, when I see the potential for helping people learn and it feels like something I want to do with my life," she said. ✳

Begin compiling a list of names, addresses, telephone numbers, job titles and people within your chosen industry who can be important information resources. This will give you a framework for the final step, conducting employer research.

Who is Hiring and How Do I Find Them?
Employer Research

Organizations, particularly private companies, spend thousands of dollars developing company literature with the expectation it will be read. Annual reports, recruiting materials, and business directories are excellent sources of information.

If you are a college graduate, you might want to contact your alumni office and ask about career services for members. If you have a career center nearby, you might want to start with company recruiting literature they might have on file. Consult the center's library or your public library for company profiles in such books as *Hoover's Handbook: Profiles of Over 500 Major Corporations,* by Gary Hoover, Alta Campbell and Patrick Spain, or *The Hidden Job Market: A Job Seekers Guide to America's 2,000 Little Known But Fastest Growing High-Tech Companies,* one of Peterson's Guides.

The easiest companies to research are those that are publicly owned, those that trade their shares on the various stock exchanges. The larger the company, the more information you will find. Look for geographic locations, names and profiles of company executives and company addresses. Industry specific directories are especially helpful here. This can be a fascinating but tedious process, so be prepared.

Look for background articles on the company and its products. In addition to the *Guide to Periodic Literature,* check for the *Business Periodicals Index, Predicasts F & S Index, Business Index, Infotrac* and other on-line services, the *Wall Street Journal* and *New York Times* indexes. If your local newspaper has an index, you might check that, too.

Publicly owned and traded companies are required to publish an annual report and these can be very informative, especially in describing new products and services, market share, corporate emphasis, and problems within the company or the industry. You'll find most of this information in the front section with the glitzy pictures. Even a quick study can give "the flavor" of a company, says David Batchelder, former chief strategist for corporate raider T. Boone Pickens and now head of his own investment firm. Madeline Aguirre (Chapter 8) learned through the annual report that the company she was going to interview with had recently purchased a food preparation company, key information that made a difference in her interview.

If the company has a local office, stop by and ask for an annual report, or better yet, the last two. If the company does not have a local facility, you may call the corporate headquarters and request these be sent to you. More important, ask them to send you copies of the most recent speeches the company's key executives have given or awards or honors they've received. Be aware this could take four to eight weeks. A quicker way to get these might be to visit a major brokerage firm and make your request. An even faster way, if you have a computer, is to use the Internet.

If the company you are interested in is a subsidiary or a division of a publicly traded company, you may have trouble finding information specific to that division. Annual reports of the parent company can be helpful if they describe the subsidiaries. Not all do. Here is where magazine articles regarding products come in handy. You also might look in *Directory of Corporate Affiliations* or *Who Owns Whom: North American Edition* for brief profiles.

In addition, *Inc.* publishes an annual survey of 500 hottest private companies. *Business Week* publishes an annual guide to the 100 fastest-growing publicly held companies. Trade magazines and newsletters are particularly helpful in providing leads on specific fields. *Soft-letter*, a Watertown, Massachusetts, newsletter on the computer-software industry, annually lists the 100 largest independent software firms, with phone numbers and growth figures.

Trade magazines also give excellent leads. For instance, in *Chain Store Age,* you might read about the unprecedented success of a retail chain. Because of its success, the company is planning to expand into new locations across the country. This expansion means the creation of new jobs.

Look in the news brief columns for the names of people who are with the companies you're interested in. See if you notice any trends: Are all the promotions occurring in one office or in one department? Is there a new department head?

If you read that John Jones left Company A and was appointed executive vice president of Company B, consider both these companies as prospective employers. Company A will be replacing Jones, and Jones quite likely will be building a new team at B.

Look for upcoming conventions and trade shows. It might be worth while to attend some seminars or meetings to make contacts.

Always read the classified section of these magazines. They're a great source of information that's difficult to get anywhere else – like current salary ranges. Many, like *Editor & Publisher* carry a "Help Wanted" section. Special issues can give you a real feel for areas that are often brushed over in regular issues.

Other information that may be published in newspapers or popular and trade magazines are contracts awarded to companies that may affect hiring. Examples might be: "Government awards contract to General Hospital to expand facilities." "Construction on new highway to begin next month." "Grand opening of new shopping mall is scheduled."

If your company is privately owned, finding information will be even more difficult. Be prepared to be creative. If it's a large enough company, you may find it listed in *Ward's Business Directory,* which provides brief data for privately owned companies whose annual sales are more than $500,000. You might find more information in one of the *Who's Who in...* series under the president's name. Or check out the *Thomas Register of American Manufacturers.* And again, check your periodical indexes.

If your company is local or regional in scope the difficulty of finding public information increases. Ask the reference librarian what information they keep on local businesses. Some keep a good deal, others practically nothing. If you live in a large city you are more likely to find local information than if you live in a smaller one. Most libraries will have an industrial directory pub-

lished by their state, giving limited information on all manufacturers within their borders. You may also want to visit your newspaper office and see if they have an index, or if you can talk with
their librarian.

Colleges and universities with business or economics departments are other good resources. They often publish information about local trends. Your local chamber of commerce may
also be helpful. Many publish a newsletter that includes stories
about its members. Some have a person specifically charged with
collecting and disseminating local economic information as well
as current information on local businesses. This could well be
your most informed source of information on local companies.

With local companies, try the direct approach – talk to someone there. With any company, large or small, public or private,
begin by asking for printed information regarding the company's
product or service. You can usually get this from the receptionist. This also gives you an opportunity to see the work site. You
might also ask for the name of the person in charge of the department you want to work in as well as the personnel director and
any other key people. The receptionist often keeps their cards at
the front desk. Better yet, ask for an organization chart, so that
you have an idea of the number and size of various departments
and who heads them. Ask if they have a newsletter. Larger companies, school systems and institutions often have to keep the
employees informed about other divisions. In-house newsletters
are a good way to get a feel for the organizational atmosphere, as
well as a sense of who the players are.

✳ *Before Barbara let her enthusiasm carry her away, I wanted to
make sure she understood she still had options to explore.*

*"Medical illustration sounds like a very viable career move for you,
but before you lock yourself in, why not get some more information on
what you might do at a museum?"*

"Back to the library," she shrugged with a sigh.

"Hold it." I reached into my bottom drawer and hauled out the telephone book. "Why don't you make a few calls to local museums instead."

"Who should I ask for?"

"Why not ask for the curator or the personnel director and ask for an informational interview?" ✳

Straight from the Horses Mouth
Informational Interviews

For really down and dirty information, set up informational interviews – interviews designed to give you information, not a job. The distinction is very important. These are most productive if you prepare well.

Begin by seeking out the highest ranking person doing the job that interests you. If you are aiming for a sales job, contact the top-ranking field sales executive in your preferred geographical area. These informational/networking interviews are the most effective way to open the doors of potential employers, because they put you in the right places at the right time to learn about potential job openings before they are ever publicized.

But beware. The sheer number of *What Color Is Your Parachute?* readers and other career changers has created a flood of information seekers. Predictably, employers and professionals have caught on and are making more careful judgments about whom to see and whom to turn away. Also strangers do not want to be job exchange bureaus. They may know about job possibilities, but are reluctant to give this information to someone whom they have just met. If you are to get a referral, you will have to earn it.

✳ *Barbara called the personnel director of the local museum of natural history and met with her within the week. Her agenda was clear. She wanted to know what positions were typically available at museums such as this, what those people did, and what their training was. She also asked to talk directly to people who held these positions.*

The personnel director was delighted in her interest because she seldom got requests for anything other than actual job interviews. They spent a fairly extensive morning touring the museum, going through the different departments, examining what each person did.

Barbara's meeting was specifically fruitful. She was particularly interested in the artists who prepared the scenes, backdrops and landscapes for the exhibits, as well as the people who were involved with exhibiting the artifacts of the museum. She talked with that particular cadre within the museum and found that they too had art backgrounds along with some science, particularly botany.

"They showed me how they had to be able to draw their scenes to complement the native plant life that you see around the animals in the dioramas."

She began to feel the same sort of fervor about exhibit preparation as she had about medical illustration. ✳

One of the best resources for informational interviews for college grads is other alumni. Being graduated from the same school tends to create instant rapport. Even if you're targeting a job in finance and there's a graduate in your area who's a marketing executive, don't discount this person, since he or she may provide you with an introduction to someone in your targeted area. Many alumni associations publish directories, providing detailed information on the whereabouts, professionally and geographically, of graduates. Even if they don't, alumni associations will sometimes provide this information.

Keep in mind the informational interview is your show, so feel free to use a list of prepared questions and to take notes, or, if given permission, tape the session. I emphasize that one of the most significant ways to ensure a successful informational interview is the preparation beforehand. The questions you ask and how you present yourself are extremely important. Some typical questions are:

- What kinds of entry level jobs do you think are good training grounds for a person entering this field now?

- What are some of the criteria that a new entrant should use when considering a specific position?
- What education/degrees/training/licenses are needed?
- What are the trends and developments in the field that you see as affecting the career of someone just entering this occupation now?
- How much time do you estimate you spend each day in the various activities of your work?
- How do people in your position interact with others in your organization?
- What are some of the problems/decisions likely to face you in a day's time? What skills are required for handling them?
- What are the most satisfying parts of your work? Most frustrating?
- What are the constraints that affect you in your work? For example, financial, legal, supervisory, policy, consumer demand?
- Would you please trace your own career path?
- Could you give me names, addresses, and telephone numbers of other people in this occupation who might be willing to talk with me about their careers as you have done?

You may find non-profit organizations are more accessible and willing to take this kind of time. In the corporate world people are not as likely to be able or willing to spend extended amounts of time with you. You might ask to take them to breakfast, lunch or for after-work drinks, but some see this as an intrusion on their personal time. It's usually best to keep work-related issues at the work site. Wherever you meet, be sure your questions are very concise, very direct, and recognize you will probably spend less than an hour of their time getting your information.

Be sure to take a resume with you, even if it is a multipurpose one. You can use it to simply and quickly share information about your background so you can move on to the task of finding out about the interviewee's background and experience.

No question, this is one of the hardest parts of the job search, and one that takes time to fine tune. Some of the things you should be looking for are the organization's age, services, competitors within the industry as a whole, growth pattern, reputation, divisions and subsidiaries, location/length of time established there, size, number of employees, revenues, new projects, and number of locations.

"Beam Me Up, Scottie!"
Using the Internet

Cyberspace is the newest networking address and you should take full advantage of it. Here you can browse through effective resume and interview techniques, job vacancies, data bases, career advice from experts, even career oriented books, and discussion groups.

On America Online you'll find the JIST Works catalog of career books, and nationally known career author Martin Yate can be found on CompuServe. There are job banks and salary surveys. America's Job Bank, maintained through the U.S. Department of Labor lists 100,000 job openings a day. You can post your resume on line, sometimes, but not always, for a fee, and reach a far broader audience than a mass mailing, and probably more effectively. You can get instructions on how to do this directly on-line or from a number of books on navigating the Internet at your library or bookstore.

"It started with techie jobs, but it's now opening up to all fields," says career columnist Joyce Lain Kennedy. "Women and minorities are coming on like gangbusters." Men see the Internet as a toy, women as a tool, she says, and 43 percent of the users are now women.

The discussion groups (sometimes referred to as forums or chat groups) allow you to ask advise, share tips and other information, and give people a feel for how you operate. They are usually broken down by subject (salaries) or fields (software programming). This can lead to job referrals, opening up the illusive "hidden job market."

Even if you don't belong to an on-line service, you may have access through your library, your alumni office, a local Internet provider. An upcoming trend is cyberspace coffee houses, where over a cappuccino, and for a hourly fee, the universe is yours.

First Things First
Decision Time

It is now time for the question I finally pose to all my clients: What do you want to do first? You will have the option throughout your life to take on many different careers, to change careers, change positions, even change industries. But what are you going to do first, and where are you going to concentrate this job? Now it's time to expand your investigations to specific organizations and job functions to develop an information network.

✱ *"I'm still having trouble making up my mind," Barbara admitted. "Both museum work and medical illustration are fascinating and fit my skills and lifestyle. I want them both." She sat back, tented her hands and closed her eyes. She spoke slowly as she worked it through.*

"I believe I have the skills and background for a museum job right now. I'm excited about that, but I don't know if I want to do that for the rest of my life." She paused again. "I'll need more training to become a medical illustrator. That's not impossible, but it will take a little while." She straighten herself. "I think I will begin by looking for jobs in museums as a scenic artist and exhibit technician."

Barbara started her search for a job as a museum exhibit technician by recontacting the artists at the natural history museum. They recommended professional publications and gave her a contact at the state professional organization. Before long she had a list of four museums that met her criteria and had open positions. Her final choice was a small museum where she was given the greatest responsibility. It was located near a university and she is now enrolled in classes leading to her certification as a medical illustrator. Then it will be decision time all over again. ✳

Researching the job market may seem tedious, but it is essential and effective. As with any learning curve, it begins slowly but the momentum builds and suddenly you achieve the Velcro effect. You become a "career consumer," choosing wisely and efficiently. To achieve this goal, keep in mind it takes work, diligence, commitment, a willingness to ask for help, time, and above all, patience. The reward is a truly satisfying career.

Resources

Career Planning

Career Crash: The End of America's Love Affair with Work, Barry Glassner, Simon & Schuster, 1994.

Complete Job Search Handbook: All the Skills You Need to Get a Good Job and Have a Good Time Doing It, The, Howard Figler, Henry Holt & Co.,1988.

Dare to Change Your Job — and Your Life, Carole Kanchier, Mastermedia Limited, 1991.

Do What You Love: The Money Will Follow: Discovering Your Right Livelihood, Marsha Sinetar, Paulist, 1989.

Finding Your Life Mission: How to Unleash That Creative Power to Live with Intention, Naomi Stephan, Stillpoint, 1989.

Global Paradox: The Bigger the World Economy, The More Powerful Its Smallest Players, John Naisbitt, Morrow, 1994.

How Not to Make It and Succeed...Life on Your Own Terms, Anna Miller-Teideman, Lifecareer Foundation, 1989.

I Could Do Anything, If I Only Knew What It Was: How to Discover What You Really Want & How to Get It, Barbara Sher & Barbara Smith, Delacorte, 1994.

JobShift: How to Prosper in a Workplace Without Jobs, William, Bridges, Addison-Wesley, 1994.

Megatrends 2000: Ten New Directions for the 1990's, John Naisbitt and Patricia Aburdene, Morrow, 1990.

New Emerging Careers: Today, Tomorrow and in the 21st Century, Norman Feingold and Martha H. Atwater, Garrett Park, 1988.

Top Professions: The 100 Most Popular, Dynamic and Profitable Careers in America Today, Nicholas Basta, Peterson's Guides, 1989.

What Color is Your Parachut? A Practical Manual for Job Hunters and Career Changers, 1995, Richard Bolles, Ten Speed Press, 1994.

Job Search

Berkeley Guide to Employment for New College Graduates, James T. Briggs, Ten Speed Press, 1984.

Dictionary of Occupational Titles, U. S. Department of Labor, JIST Works, 1991.

Encyclopedia of Associations, 1996, Gale Research Co., 1995.

Guerrilla Tactics in the Job Market, Tom Jackson, Bantam Books, 1993.

Hoover's Handbook of Emerging Companies, 1994-1995: Profiles of America's Most Exciting Growth Enterprises, Patrick J. Spain, Reference Press, 1994.

Hoover's Handbook of American Business, Gary Hoover, Alta Campbell and Patrick Spain, The Reference Press, 1994.

Interview for Success: A Practical Guide to Increasing Job Interviews, Offers & Salaries, Caryl Rae and Ronald Krannich, Impact Publications, 1993.

Jobs 95: By Careers, By Industry, By Region, Ross & Kathryn Petras, Simon & Schuster, 1993.

Knock 'em Dead: The Ultimate Job Seeker's Handbook, Martin Yate, Bob Adams Press, 1994.

National Directory of Corporate Training Programs, Ray Bard and Susan Elliott, Doubleday Publishing, 1988.

Perfect Cover Letter, The, Richard Beatty, John Wiley & Sons, 1989.

Perfect Resume, The, Max Eggert, Random House, 1994.

Quick Job Hunting Map for Beginners, The, Richard Bolles & Victoria B. Zenoff, Ten Speed Press, 1977.

Resume Catalog: 200 Damn Good Examples, The, Yana Parker, Ten Speed Press, 1988.

Electronic Job Search

Access...FCO On-Line, Federal Research Service, Inc., 243 Church Street N.W., Vienna, VA 22180.

America Online, (800) 827-6364.

American Mathematical Society, gopher <e-math.ams.com>

American Physiological Society, gopher <gopher.uth-tmc.edu>

Career Doctors Bulletin Board Service, Executive Directions, 2 Penn Plaza, Suite 1185, New York, NY 10121.

Career Link Worldwide, (800) 453-3350.

Career Network, (800) 229-6599.

Catapult The, http://www.wm.edu/catapult/catapult.html

Classacomputerfields, (800) 753-4223.

Classifacts, North American Classifacts, 50 South Steel Street, Suite 222, Denver, CO 80209.

Computerworld Careers On-Line, P.O. Box 880, Framingham, MA 01701.

Contractor's Exchange, (415) 334-7393.

Discussions about job search, interviews, researching firms, etc., <misc.obs.misc>

E-Span, (800) 682-2901.

Electronic Resumes for the New Job Market: Resumes that Work for You, 24 Hours a Day, Peter D. Weddle, Impact, 1994.

Employment Opportunities and Job Resources on the Internet, http://www.wpi.edu/Depts/Library/jobguide/index.html (The Riley Guide)

Federal Job Opportunities Board, (912)757-3100 or telnet <job.mail.opm.gov> or gopher <gopher.dartmouth.edu>

FedWorld, (703)321-8020 or telnet <fedworld.gov>

Gopher Jewels, gopher <cwis.usc.edu> (Gateways to job-listing services, the U.S. Department of Labor *Occupational Outlook Handbook* and listings of state employment offices.)

Hooked Up Get Hired! The Internet Job Search Revolution, Joyce Lain Kennedy & Thomas J. Morrow, John P. Wiley, 1995.

InterAction (American Council for Voluntary International Action), ia@interaction.org, gopher or http://www.vita.org/iaction/iaction.html

International Career and Emmployment Network, http://www.indiana.edu/~intlcent/icen/index.html

Job Ads USA, Militran, Inc., 1255 Drummers Lane, Suite 306, Wayne, PA 19087.

Job postings collected from a variety of online sources, <misc.jobs.offered>

Job postings nationwide, <bizjobs.offered>

Jobtrac, 6856 Arboreal Drive, Dallas, TX 75231.

Jobtrak, 1990 Westwood Boulevard, Suite 260, Los Angeles, CA 90025.

LA Online, 332 Hermosa Avenue, Suite 7, Hermosa Beach, CA 90254.

JobWeb, <http://www.jobweb.org>

Monster Board, <http://www.monster.com/> (An interactive data base for listing and locating job opportunities.)

Networking Careers On-Line, (800) 622-1108.

On-Line Career Fair, Response Technologies Corporation, Two Campton Commons, Campton, NH 03223.

Online Career Center (OCC), http://occ.com/

On-Line Job Search Companion, The, James C. Gonyea, McGraw-Hill, 1994.

Online Opportunities Bulletin Board, (215) 873-7170.

OT Source, on-line service for occupational therapists, (800) 377-8555.

Society for Technical Communication, 901 North Stuart Street, Suite 904, Arlington, VA 22203.

University of Minnesota College of Education's Job-Search Bulletin Board, gopher <rodent.dix.umn.edu-11119>

Working and Living Overseas, http://www.magi.com/~issi/

Company Research

ABI/Inform, UMI. (Also available on CD-ROM.)

America's Corporate Families, Dun's Marketing Services, 1993.

Best Companies for Women, The, Baila Zeitz, Simon & Schusster, 1988.

Business Periodicals Index, Wilson, 1994. (Also available on CD-ROM.)

Companies That Care, Hal Morgan & Kerry Tucker, 1991.

Companies With a Conscience: Intimate Portraits of Twelve Firms That Make a Difference, Mary Scott & Howard Rothman, Carol Publishing Group, 1992.

Directory of Corporate Affiliations, U. S. Private, National Register Publishing Co., 1994.

Directory of Foreign Firms Operating in the U.S., World Trade, 1994.

Everybody's Business: A Field Guide to the 400 Leading Companies in America, Milton Moskowitz, Doubleday, 1990.

Million Dollar Directory: Top 50,000 Companies, Dun's Marketing Services, 1993.

Predicasts F & S Index (Also available on CD-ROM.)

Reference Book of Corporate Managements: America's Corporate Leaders, Dun's Marketing Service, 1993. (Also available on CD-ROM.)

Standard Directory of Advertisers, Standard Rate & Data Service, 1995.

Standard & Poor's Industry Surveys

Standard and Poor's Register of Corporations, Directors, and Executives. (Also available on CD-ROM.)

Thomas Register of American Manufacturers, 1995, Rector Press, 1994. (Also available on CD-ROM.)

U. S. Industrial Outlook 1994: An Almanac of Industry, Technology & Services, U.S. Department of Commerce, Reference Press, 1993.

Ward's Business Directory, Gale Research Inc., 1994. (Also available on CD-ROM.)

Who's Who in Finance and Industry, 1994-1995, Marquis, 1993.

Industry Specific

Advertising Career Directory, Ronald W. Fry, Career Press, 1992.

Almanac of International Jobs & Careers: A Guide to Over 1001 Employers, Ronald and Caryl Krannich, Impact Publications, 1994.

Alternative Careers for Teachers, Sandy Pollack, Harvard Common Press, 1984.

American Almanac of Jobs and Salaries,1994-1995, The, John W. Wright, Avon, *1993.*

Book Publishing Career Directory, Ronald W. Fry, Visible Ink Press, 1992.

Breaking into Broadcasting, Donna Pearlman, Bonus Books, 1986.

Career Opportunities in Advertising & Public Relations, Shelly Field, Facts on File Publications, 1990.

Career Opportunities in Art: A Comprehensive Guide to the Exciting Careers Open to You in Art, Susan Haubenstock and David Joselit, Facts on File Publications, 1988.

Career Opportunities in the Food and Beverage Industries, Barbara Sims-Bell, Facts on File, 1994.

Career Opportunities in Television, Cable & Radio, Maxine and Robert Reed, Facts on File Publications, 1991.

Career Opportunities in the Music Industry, Shelly Field, Facts on File Publications, 1990.

Careers for Bookworms and Other Literary Types, Marjorie Eberts and Margaret Gisler, VGM Career Horizons, 1990.

Careers for Good Samaritans & Other Humanitarian Types, Marjorie Eberts and Margaret Gisler, VGM Career Horizons, 1991.

Careers for Sports Nuts & Other Athletic Types, William Heitzmann, VGM Career Horizons, 1991.

Careers in Communications, Shonan Noronha, VGM Career Books, 1993.

Careers in Education, Roy Edelfelt, VGM Career Books, 1988.

Careers in Government, Mary E. Pits, NTC Publishing Group, 1994.

Careers in Health Care, Barbara Swanson, NTC Publications, 1989.

Careers in Medicine: Traditional and Alternative Opportunities, Donald T. Rucher and Martin D. Keller, Garrett Park Press, 1990.

Careers Working With Animals, Humane Society of the United States, Acropolis Books, Ltd., 1979.

Companies That Care, Hal Morgan & Kerry Tucker.

Complete Guide to Environmental Careers, The, The CEIP Fund, Inc., Island Press, 1989.

Creative Careers: Real Jobs in Glamour Fields, Gary Blake and Robert Bly, John Wiley & Sons, 1985.

Developing a Career in Sports, Greg Cylkowski, Movement Publications, 1988.

Developing a Lifelong Contract in the Sports Marketplace, Greg Cylkowski, Global Sports Productions, 1992.

Directory of Art Publishers, Book Publishers and Record Companies, Constance Franklin, Directors Guild Publishers.

Directory of Fine Art Representatives & Corporations Collecting Art, Constance Franklin, Directors Guild Publishers and The Consultant Press, 1990.

Finding a Job in the Non-Profit Sector, William Wade, The Taft Group, 1991.

Flying High in Travel: A Complete Guide to Careers in the Travel Industry, Karen Ruben, John Wiley & Sons, 1992.

Food Work, Jobs in the Food Industry and How to Get Them, Barbara Sims-Bell, Advocacy Press, 1993.

Good Works: A Guide to Careers in Social Change, Ralph Nader, Barricade Books, 1993.

Great Careers for People Interested in How Things Work, Peter Richardson & Bob Richardson, Gale, 1993.

Great Careers: The Fourth of July Guide to Careers, Internships, and Volunteer Opportunities in the Non-Profit Sector, Cottrell Devon Smith, Garrett Park Press.

Growing Minds: On Becoming a Teacher, Herbert Kohn, Harper & Row, 1989.

Hidden Job Market 1995: A Job Seekers Guide to America's 2,000 Little Known But Fastest Growing High-Tech Companies, The, Kitty Colton & Michele Fetterolf, Peterson's Guides, 1994.

High Tech Jobs for Non-Tech Grads, Mark O'Brien, Prentice Hall, 1986.

How To Break into the Film Business: The Production Assistant's Handbook, Jeff Alves, Players Press, 1991.

How to Get a Job in Radio: Proven Techniques to Save Time, Money, & Get You on the Airwaves, Steve Stucker, Stucker Productions, 1990.

How to Get a Job in Sports: The Guide to Finding the Right Sports Career, John Taylor, Macmillan, 1992.

How to Get a Job on a Cruise Ship, Don Kennedy, Career Source, 1991.

How to Get a Job With a Cruise Line — Travel — Romance, How to Sail Around the World on Luxury Cruise Ships and Get Paid for It, Mary Fallon Miller, Ticket to Adventure, 1994.

International Jobs: Where They Are & How To Get Them, Eric Kocher, Addison-Wesley Publishing Co., Inc., 1993.

Jobs in Paradise: The Definitive Guide to Exotic Jobs Everywhere, Jeffery M. Maltzman, Harper & Row, 1993.

Liberal Education and Careers Today, Howard Figler, Garrett Park Press, 1989.

Magazine Careers Directory, Ronald W. Fry, Visible Ink Press, 1993.

Music Business, The, Dick Weissman, Crown Publications, 1990.

National Directory of Arts Internships, Warren Christensen, The National Network for Artist Placement, 1991.

National Trade & Professional Associations of the United States, John Russell, Columbia Books, Inc., 1993.

Outdoor Careers: Exploring Occupations in Outdoor Fields, Ellen Shenk, Stackpole, 1992.

Passport to Overseas Employment: 100,000 Job Opportunities Abroad, Dale Chambers, Prentice Hall Press, 1990.

Professional's Job Finder, Daniel Lauber, Planning Communications, 1992.

Profitable Careers in Non-Profit, William Lewis and Carol Milano, John Wiley & Sons, 1987.

Public Relations: Career Directory, A Practical One-Step Guide to Getting a Job in Public Relations, Bradley J. Morgan, Gale, 1993.

Radio & Television Career Directory: A Practical One-Stop Guide to Getting a Job, Bradley J. Morgan, Visible Ink Press, 1993.

Schools Abroad of Interest to Americans, Porter Sargent Staff, Porter Sargent Publications, 1991.

Space Careers, Charles Sheffield and Carol Rosin, First Quill Edition, 1984.

T. V. News: Building a Career in Broadcast Journalism, Ray White, Butterworth-Heinemann, 1989.

Television Careers: A Guide to Breaking and Entering, Linda Guess Farris, Buy The Book Enterprises, 1995.

Travel & Hospitality Career Directory, Ronald W. Fry, Visible Ink Press, 1992.

THE PROFESSIONAL SELF MODEL
A THREE-STEP PROCESS

The Professional Self is an attitude, created through knowledge, focused through research and packaged to sell.

STEP 1
PERSONAL ASSESSMENT

Explore your skills, interests, work values and personality style to know yourself and what you are capable of.

STEP 2
EXPLORING & RESEARCHING THE JOB MARKET

Learn to identify global and national issues that point to expanding and contracting markets, identify expanding industries in your fields of interest, specific organizations in those industries, and positions you can actually apply for.

STEP 3
DEVELOPING YOUR MARKETING TOOLS

Learn to create dynamite resumes, interview techniques that make you stand out, and negotiating strategies to get the most out of the job. Discover how to support these with correspondence that sells. Learn how to generate industry specific materials that sell your ability.

Based on *Unlimited Options: Career Strategies to Last a Lifetime*, by Lily Maestas, M.S.W., and Lorelei Snyder, copyright © 1996 by Prosperity Press.

Developing Your Marketing Tools

- Create "value-adding" correspondence that gets you noticed and remembered.

- Dress up your raw data to showcase a star performer.

- Develop industry-specific and position-targeted resumes.

- Present yourself as a self-confident candidate at any interview.

- Practice the steps for successful negotiation.

- Feel the power of your Professional Self.

7 Correspondence that Sells
Who to write to, why, when and how

> *"As you progress through this job search, remember words create a thousand pictures."*

Sooner or later you are going to have to put pen (or word processor) to paper. Effective letters are pivotal job marketing tools. The written message gives the potential employer an insight into how you communicate, organize and present your thoughts and quite frankly, how well you write. Every job search takes on a personality of its own and requires its own specific correspondence. You know you can't get away from cover letters and thank you notes, but there are other pieces of correspondence you may overlook, such as:

- Clarification letters
- Acceptance/rejection letters
- Query letters
- Questionnaires
- Industry specific materials

Cover Letters

A cover letter with your resume is obligatory. Whether your letter gets read or not the message you send is that you know what the appropriate procedure is. Sending a resume without a cover letter is like serving someone a piece of cake. Not everyone eats the frosting, but everyone likes to see it. They are especially important if your resume will be scanned.

Your cover letter is a sales presentation. It's your initial opportunity to set the stage for your resume, and to tune the employer in to why you should be considered. It needs to catch the reader's attention, persuade them of your value, and convince them to act. It is a brief, well written introduction to your resume.

I always advise following the 1-2-1 approach. That is, your cover letter should consist of three paragraphs, the first about one inch long, or no more than six typed lines, the second about two inches, and the third no longer than one inch, or a total of about twenty-four typed lines. This forces you to write short, concise letters. Your statements must be clear, definitive and to the point.

The basic message in your first paragraph is: "This is who I am and why I am writing you this letter." Try to be more creative than "Regarding your ad for an administrative assistant," but also avoid the other extreme such as: "I am a dynamic go-getter seeking a high-profile position with a fast growing organization." You might look at something like, "After a successful and rewarding five years in the computer industry, I have now set my sights on entering the accounting field."

The second paragraph is what I call the "meat and potatoes section." The information does not reiterate your resume but rather enhances it and encourages the reader to turn to it. You may want to expand on your reasons for pursuing this particular organization or share some bit of information you know about the company. Try to express yourself in no more than twelve typed lines. You might choose three aspects of your work experience, achievements, or abilities that demonstrate how well suited you are for the job, and bullet them for emphasis.

If you are a little shy of the job qualifications, but you have comparable experience, here is the place to emphasize it.

The third paragraph is the "action and closing." Tell them what you are planning to do next, but try to avoid the, "I look forward to hearing from you" business. Request an application. Suggest a meeting time. You might try something like: "I'll telephone you in a week to discuss employment opportunities," or "I look forward to an opportunity to further discuss with you personally my qualifications for the position." Be sure to let them know how to reach you and when it's easiest.

Again, brevity and clarity are the order of the day. Here is an example of the 1-2-1 approach in action.

✳ *Lucille had known since she was eight years old that she wanted to live in New Mexico. That was the first summer her grandparents included her on their annual trek to the American Southwest. She looked forward to their weekly excursions onto the Indian reservations where her grandfather volunteered at the medical clinic and her grandmother took her on walks with the tribal women to explore cave dwellings and ruins.*

Later Lucille returned to New Mexico to attend college where she majored in journalism and Native American studies. In her senior year she spent a semester at the Los Angeles Times on an internship.

When she graduated she was determined to remain in New Mexico and to work with the Bureau of Indian Affairs. Here is the cover letter she included with her resume when she applied for a job she unearthed while researching a story during her internship. ✳

Dear Ms. Miller:

As a recent graduate from the University of New Mexico with a double major in Journalism and Native American Studies, I am seeking a position that will utilize my academic and practical experience. I believe the position you mentioned in the Los Angeles Times 10/22/89 article provides for such an opportunity.

As my resume indicates, I have held a variety of positions writing for the university newspaper as well as professional internship experience with the Los Angeles Times. My interest in working with the Bureau of Indian Affairs and specifically Corporate Communications came after tracking a story for the LA Times in which you highlighted the work being done by your department in linking major corporations with NativeAmerican tribes in the preservation of historical artifacts. I believe my credentials will be of intetest to you.

I have enclosed a copy of my resume for your review and look forward to the possibility of employment with you. I will call your office on Monday. I would like to schedule a meeting with you on Thursday or Friday, if that would be convenient. I look forward to our time together.

Sincerely

Lucille Anderson
Enclosure

If at all possible, your cover letter should be addressed to someone, not just to a title or an office. It is too easy for your letter and any other material you send with it to end up in the round file unread if you do not mail it directly to someone by name. This is where your employer research pays off. You may be able to get the proper person simply by calling the company and asking for the name of the personnel manager. If you are stuck with responding to a box number, avoid the standard "Dear Sir:" and try something more neutral, such as "Hello!" or "Good Morning!"

Thank You Letters

You write thank you letters because it is the right thing to do. Think about it. You have asked someone to fill out a questionnaire you developed. Perhaps you conducted an informational interview with them and they gave you the name of a friend in another company to contact. You asked someone to write you a letter of recommendation or to serve as a reference during your job search. You had an especially good interview experience with a personnel director and want to make contact again and express continued interest in the position. In each case, someone has given you something.

Second, you write thank you's because they are effective marketing pieces. Studies show that the highest correlation between those looking for work and those who get job offers is the thank you letter. What's more, nurturing the relationship may keep your contact interested in aiding your job search through leads, contacts, and maybe even an offer down the road. One of the major vehicles for conducting a successful job search is networking. An important way to make sure networking happens is through the liberal use of thank you letters. It is important to build bridges and keep in touch. Letting people know you appreciate their efforts on your behalf makes them feel the time they took out of their day was worthwhile. Being told you are appreciative is a major reason for people to continue to take an active interest in your success.

Besides, writing thank you notes lets the recipient know your mother brought you up right.

Thank you notes are most often short and hand written, if your writing is legible. An effective thank you can be as simple as this:

Dear Mr. Powell:

I would like to take a minute of your time to thank you for the interview for the graphic design position with your firm this past Monday. As a result of our discussion I am more certain than ever that there is a place for me at Melmen Advertising.

Sincerely,

Barbara Bailey

Thank you letters should recall for the receiver their part in your job search and require careful thought and preparation. This may dictate a longer, more detailed letter.

✳ *When Leigh composed her thank you letter for a job interview, it took a full four hours, in addition to the research it refers to. Although somewhat longer than usual, it did the trick. Upper management was impressed with the effort that went into it, and decided to take a chance on her, even though she had no direct experience in sales.* ✳

Dear Mr. Ware:

Thank you for the extensive time you took with me last week. I thoroughly enjoyed the morning. I believe working with your company would be an exciting and rewarding challenge.

Since our meeting I have discussed the leasing business here in Santa Barbara with some of my chamber of commerce contacts. Their comments confirm that there is definitely an expanding market for this business, but also noted that the competition is keen. Rates vary but little, and approvals can take as little as one day. Where approvals are difficult to get, the circumstance is usually one of a slow-pay history, and I wonder how your company treats such situations?

While many of the existing leasing companies provide sales training programs for their customers such as you described, few do it on a regular, consistent basis. Indeed when I asked, "What would create company loyalty for you?" the answer was unanimously "Service!" I believe you have a winner there. Other comments included, "My customer gets quick approval and I get quick payment."

If your sales expectations are accurate, I can see clearly they will not be achievable without a great deal of dedicated hard work, with an astute eye toward prompt and good service. I believe I can deliver that.

I would look forward to spending two weeks with you learning the business and the territory. During that time I would expect to identify at least ten key manufacturing areas for initial pursuit. I am confident by then I will be well qualified to "solo."

Yours very truly,

Leigh Kilbourne

Your appreciation is what should be the central theme of any thank you letter. If you can, it is also a good idea to let them know the outcome of the job search and the part they played in making it successful. If the person they referred you to in another company eventually offered you a position, tell them that. If their responses on the questionnaire provided you with added insight into a particular industry, tell them so. If your interview went well and there were one or two highlights that you can recall, mention them. But first and foremost you are writing to say thank you for taking the time to be a part of something that was very important to you.

✳*When one of her references gave her a personal referral, Amanda followed up with great results. Here's what she wrote:* ✳

Dear Esther:

Thank you so much for your wonderful letter of recommendation. Your comments were very kind and addressed some of my most pertinent work related experience. This job search has certainly been exciting and filled with unexpected surprises. The most memorable being your referral to your sorority sister at Athens Industries. As a result of that referral and my follow up I have been offered an engineering position with Athens! One which I think I am going to accept.

Your active participation in my job search has made a tremendous difference. In the future I hope to be able to model your generous example with another "talented young professional" that may one day seek my assistance.

Thank you once again for your efforts.

Sincerely,

Amanda Madison

Clarification Letters

Cover letters and thank you's are musts, but there are other opportunities where a good letter will make a difference.

The clarification letter is most often used by someone moving up or laterally within the same organization, or by someone who has taken on a work assignment for a limited time. Usually these kinds of work assignments involve extra compensation for the additional work responsibilities. Salary negotiations and upgrading of benefits packages also make clarification letters necessary.

The letter provides written documentation of the changes you have agreed to make as you understand them. If there is confusion between you and your employer regarding these changes, the clarification letter usually identifies them early and avoids misunderstandings down the road. Differing recollections or information that does not get passed on to a new supervisor can be devastating.

✱ *Joan had worked as a Social Worker at Community Hospital for seven years. During that time she developed particular expertise in the area of discharge planning for elderly stroke patients. The steady increase in the numbers of these patients finally demanded a reorganization of the department without, of course, increasing staff. The hospital administration asked Joan to supervise the project. She was excited by the opportunity to "see that it gets done right."*

In her acceptance letter she wanted to make it clear that this temporary work assignment would require her to relinquish some of her current responsibilities, but that she expected to resume her original position when it was finished. The letter Joan wrote outlined the pa-

*rameters of the agreement with time lines, salary adjustments and po-
sition title changes. There was very little left to the imagination, which is
exactly what Joan wanted.* ✳

Dear Mr. Baldwin:

*I am excited about the opportunity to develop and implement a new dis-
charge planning component. I appreciate your confidence in me. To be
sure I am clear regarding our discussion last week, I would like to outline
for both of us my understanding regarding this reorganization.*

1. *On March 16, I will assume the responsibility of Project Manager for
   the reorganization of the Discharge Planning Component of the Social
   Work Service at the hospital. The project is estimated to last six months
   and will include the completion of the following tasks:*

   A. *Evaluation of all positions within the component including appro-
      priate recommendations for reclassification and salary adjustments.*

   B. *Review of the current budget with recommendations regarding ef-
      fective use of resources.*

   C. *Review and modification of the current referral system to accommo-
      date the increase in elderly discharge planning assignments. The
      change in procedure will reflect the need for increased interaction
      with geriatric referral sources within the Greater Los Angeles area.*

   D. *In an effort to minimize disruption of services and promote coopera-
      tion, weekly updates and input from the staff will be crucial. A list of
      the scheduled meetings for the next three months is attached.*

2. *As a result of this project, I will be relieved of my caseload assignments
   effective immediately. Said responsibilities will be reinstated upon
   completion of the project. In order to complete this project in a timely
   manner, you have agreed to provide me with two additional support
   staff personnel to handle the increase in paperwork and ensure proper
   documentation of procedures.*

3. *During the next six months my salary will reflect a thousand dollars a
   month increase which will terminate at the completion of this project.*

My title will be Project Manager and I will report directly to Harriet Briggs, Chief Administrative Officer of the hospital. The final report will be due three weeks after completion of the project and will be submitted directly to the Board of Directors of the hospital.

I am looking forward to the challenge this opportunity represents and am confident the resulting recommendations will make a tremendous difference in discharge planning thus ensuring higher quality services to our patients. I am delighted to have this opportunity and would like to thank you again for the assignment.

If you have any questions regarding the above outline, please talk with me at your earliest convenience.

Sincerely,

Joan Graham, MSW

Keep in mind, it is in your best interest to take the initiative and outline for your employer what you see the changes will be in your relationship with the organization. Don't wait until the information is presented to you. If it is incorrect, you are then put in the awkward position of having to correct your boss, whereas, if you outline the changes first, you present yourself as a conscientious employee attempting to avoid conflict.

Acceptance/Rejection Or Counter Offer Letters

Once you are in a position to write an acceptance/rejection or a counter-offer letter, you know all your hard work has paid off. Congratulations! You hold in your hand a job description and title, salary offer, and a benefits package and your reply is eagerly awaited.

It's always best to give yourself a few days to think it over, even if you are sure you will accept the position. Why? Most important for me is the opportunity to bask in the glow of success. Very seldom do we have an opportunity to feel this good about something, and I think you should take advantage of this moment purely for its own sake!

A more down-to-earth reason is to allow time to really review the job responsibilities, travel requirements, salary and benefits to see what you are actually buying into.

✱ *In some cases it's easy. After conducting a thorough job search in a number of industries, Bill, a laboratory chemist, was delighted when he was offered a position requiring the use of his scientific training to help develop solutions to world hunger. He felt his personal values were closely aligned with those of the organization and looked forward to the "team project" approach exhibited in the laboratory. In accepting the position he wanted to give the employer some indication of his enthusiasm for the organization.* ✱

Dear Mr. Silverman:

This is a follow up to our conversation last Friday regarding the position as Food Chemist for Biotech. After reviewing the information you sent over by messenger, I am pleased to accept your offer of employment starting March 15.

Working to provide alternative food sources for drought stricken areas is, for me, an excellent way to use my technical training and provide some possible solutions for international hunger problems. I am looking forward to my association with the other chemists I met while on the plant tour last week.

I am returning your copy of the signed contract. I will wait for your orientation materials to be sent at a later date. I look forward to a productive and satisfying relationship with Biotech.

Sincerely,

William Owens

✳ *On the other hand, Jane was faced with tactfully rejecting an offer from a hospital that had shown obvious interest and enthusiasm for her. During her job search, she had narrowed her industries of interest to health care and insurance. At this juncture, she had received two offers, one in each field, both attractive. However, in her research she learned of a great deal of internal strife in the department in which she would work at the hospital, resulting in high turnover.*

While she liked Valley Hospital and thought that some day she might like to work there, she was not interested in accepting this current offer. Here's how she handled it: ✳

Dear Ms. Evans:

After careful consideration of your offer of employment as an accountant, I have decided not to accept at this time. This has been a difficult decision on my part as you presented some interesting professional challenges. However, an offer from another industry appears to more closely match my career needs at this point.

I continue to hold Valley Hospital in high regard and would consider employment with you should the right opportunity present itself at a later date. Thank you for the time you spent with me during this interview process and I wish you the best of luck.

Sincerely,

Jane Forrest, CPA

Some offers are not so simple. You may want to negotiate for a different benefits package, or clarify your responsibilities, or make a counter proposal. The time to do this is before you sign a contract, not afterward. Most employers will want to hurry the acceptance process along since negotiating with you is not seen as in their best interests. Remember their main objective is to hire the best employee for the least amount of money.

✳ *After reviewing the job offer Andy was not quite satisfied, so he made a counter offer. Here is his letter:* ✳

Dear Ms. Sandstrom:

I was excited to receive your offer of employment last week. The thought of working for Johnson Industries in San Diego is appealing and I look forward to a positive resolution to some of the disparities we discussed in our phone conversation last week.

I want to assure you that I am very interested in the position and the job activities even though the particulars of employment have yet to be agreed upon. In an effort to move in that direction I am proposing the following changes in your salary and benefits offer.

1. *I would like to propose that we share the relocation costs equally and forgo for this year your funding of my membership in the American Public Health Association. My membership is current and renewal will not be necessary until a year from now. The money you have allocated to cover that expenditure could be used to cover your portion of the moving expenses.*

2. *I understand that the salary you quoted is non-negotiable. I would like to suggest that we shorten the time before my first performance review to six months as opposed to a year. In that time I am confident you will have had a chance to observe my work and we can discuss salary options at that time.*

If these two revisions in your proposal meet with your approval, I see no reason for me to delay accepting your offer of employment. I look forward to hearing from you.

Sincerely,

Andrew Miller

* Take note that in the counter offer Andy clearly states his desire to accept the job, but the conditions of employment are not quite what he had in mind. In both of his proposals he mentions what he wants changed and offers reasonable alternatives. He becomes part of the solution as opposed to just presenting the company with a problem. It *presents a positive, problem solving, interactive approach to the situation rather than a defensive one.* ✳

Query Letters

Query letters are useful if you are conducting an out-of-the-area job search, are interested in a particular aspect of an industry or as a prelude to an informational interview. Your query letter is one step in the process of matching what you discovered from your personal assessment with what is available in the market place. Your primary purpose is to get your contacts to give you information and advice, refer you to others, and remember you. Query letters are constructed to be non-threatening to the reader and demonstrate a genuine desire to gather information only. If it comes across as a disguised attempt to gain employment or secure a job interview, you blew it.

Key things to remember here. Make sure you include an estimate of the amount of time you think the interview will take, when you will contact them for an appointment and be specific as to the nature of the interview.

✳ *Jonathan (Chapter 2) sent out the following letter to fifteen people in the entertainment and music industry. Of out those, three, or twenty percent, agreed to speak with him.* ✳

Dear Mr. Marquez:

After a significant amount of research into the music and entertainment industry I have selected you as one of the fifteen people whose opinion I am interested in obtaining. I am currently working with a career counselor exploring alternative career options for myself. Having entered the insurance industry as an actuary immediately upon graduation from college, I am now ready to move into my next career and am looking for ways to combine my professional experience with my life long interest in music.

I am seriously considering making a career change into this industry. As this is a major departure for me, I am fully aware it will require additional education and training on my part. Before I make that commitment I want to know from those who know best, the variety of positions available within the industry for someone with my academic and professional qualifications. With this information I will be able to construct an efficient and effective plan of action.

I am aware that pressures on your time are great, but I would appreciate it if you would schedule just one-half hour with me to share your expertise and personal observations on this matter. The information I gather will help me to better focus my efforts.

I appreciate your consideration of my request and will call you next week to discuss a convenient time for you. Thank you in advance for your help. I look forward to talking with you.

Sincerely,

Jonathan Banks

Questionnaire

A questionnaire allows you to ask standardized questions and gather consistent information from a variety of sources without having to interview each of the participants directly.

This is an extremely useful tool if you keep clear about your objective, which is to gather information that will help you narrow and focus your job search. In designing your questionnaire be brief. It is better to design yes/no, or multiple choice questions. Essay questions are time consuming and few are willing to take the time to write down lots of information. More likely they will put it aside in a "To Do Later" file, and you know what happens to that. You can include a request for comments after some of your questions, but only as an option. Your questionnaire should take no more than ten minutes to fill out. Less than five is even better. Keep the length to no more than two pages.

The content of the questions is entirely up to you and should be based on the kind of information you need. Make sure to include a cover letter with your questionnaire and a self-addressed stamped envelope for easy return. Need we say it's important to follow up all replies with a thank you letter?

✻ For as long as she could remember, Janice had spent her summers either attending or working at summer camps, and now, as she approached graduation, she wanted to continue in that field.

One of our annual campus events is a Camp Day. Directors from over 50 summer camps come to interview students for summer counselor and activity coordinator positions. I encouraged Janice to develop a questionnaire to send to the participating directors to fill out and return to her on the day of the event. In the questionnaire she asked about their own career paths, educational training and work experience that gave them the credentials needed for a director's position.

By and large people like to talk about their careers and how they got there. It makes a good impression when someone wants to learn from their experience and it makes them more likely to take an interest in answering and returning the survey. In a relatively short time not only was Janice able to get information from a large number of people in positions exactly like the one she herself wanted, she also made initial contact with these directors in a very positive way. ✻

CAMP DIRECTOR INFORMATION QUESTIONNAIRE

Hi! My name is Janice Appleton, and I am a student here at UCSB. I have been considering a career as a Camp Director of outdoor and/or summer camps. At our career center, I could not find specific information for this type of job. I am hoping that your knowledge and experience can help me out. Please take just five minutes to answer the following questions. Thank you.

1) *How did you first get involved in camps and/or recreation?*
   - ☐ *As a counselor*   ☐ *Transferred from a related field*
   - ☐ *As a participant*   ☐ *Other_____*

2) *What specifics helped you to get this job?*
   - ☐ *Licenses*   ☐ *Special classes*
   - ☐ *Internships*   ☐ *Former positions*
   - ☐ *Volunteer work*   ☐ *Other_____*

3)   *How many hours a week do you spend at this position? Could*
      you break these hours down into specific categories? (bookkeep-
      ing, publicity, hiring personnel, supervision, etc.)

4)   *What future opportunities could this job open up for you? (vari-*
      ous other jobs, different fields, higher education)

5)   *What is your educational background in terms of school, degree,*
      studies, etc.?

6)   *Please describe your camp.*
      *Camper Demographics*_____
      *Camper Population*_____ *Staff*_____
      *Average Session*_____ *Setting*_____

      Activities
      ☐ *Swimming*   ☐ *Tennis*   ☐ *Horseback riding*
      ☐ *Crafts*   ☐ *Dancing*   ☐ *Rifle range*
      ☐ *Campfires*   ☐ *Camping*   ☐ *Canoeing*
      ☐ *Sailing*   ☐ *Religious*   ☐ *Specialized skills*
      ☐ *Other (please specify)* _____

7)   *What professional associations do you belong to and why?*

8)   *May I write to you if I have further questions? Y*_____ *N*_____
Name   _____
Title   _____
Camp   _____
Address _____
          _____

Industry Specific Materials

Some industries require very specific documentation of your work. Journalists, writers, editors and those involved with the written word will need to submit writing samples. When a friend of mine wanted to become a news reporter, she submitted clippings of published articles she had written for a community theater group and as public relations chair for the local League of Women Voters. Architects, graphic designers, artists, and people involved in advertising will usually have to submit a portfolio of their work. Those in the broadcast industries will need to submit tapes.

How do you gather this kind of material if you are still in the process of job changing or have never worked in the industry? Take a look around you. Where can you get the experience you need for your new career on an unpaid basis? What needs doing in your favorite charity? What about your church? Internships and volunteer work not only provide you with the means for creating this material, it will help you establish a track record in your new profession.

The rule of first impressions applies to your portfolio as well as your appearance. Include only your best work, presented in the most professional format you can create.

As you progress through this job search remember words create a thousand pictures. The written word calls attention to your assets, recalls your uniqueness, reiterates your strengths, and demands a response. It makes people feel good about knowing you. Don't neglect it. Make your pen (or keyboard) a well-used power tool on your job-search work bench.

8 Creating A Convincing Resume
Use your database to repackage yourself

> *"As you progress through this job search, remember words create a thousand pictures."*

The job of a resume is to get you interviews. A winning resume package gives the employer a basic understanding of your qualifications for the job, a curiosity about who you are and a desire to know more about you. It inspires the employer to invite you for an interview.

A good resume –
- Attracts attention.
- Creates interest.
- Describes accomplishments.
- Provokes action (interviews).

It should –
- Emphasize pertinent data.
- Communicate job related skills.
- Create the desired image.

A good resume has –
- A clearly stated Career Objective.
- A skills listing directly related to the career objective.
- A listing of pertinent work and experience history.
- A listing of education and training.

For a career changer, the key is to identify what you want to move to, and then create a resume that points in that direction. You may need to spend some time identifying your interests, skills and experiences, and finding a good match for them in the new workplace.

✻ *After three years on the fast track with a major retailer, Ellen Fairchild was ready to toss it away in favor of a new career, but she felt locked in, trapped. The feeling is not unusual. Looking at her resume, her experience, training and accomplishments pointed in only one direction, and she wanted to go in another.*

"Way back in my freshman year, I stopped in at the college radio station. I'd never been in a radio station before, but Bingo!" Her fists exploded. "I thought, 'Wow! This is for me.' There was a sign up sheet for volunteers, and from then on I was hooked."

She spent all her spare time at the station, always eager for another experience. Now at this current crossroad, her goal was to become an on-air radio personality.

"Why didn't you go into radio right out of college?" I asked.

"It seemed too frivolous," she told me. "Everyone was so sure I'd be such a terrific manager, it seemed silly not to take advantage of the retail opportunity I had." She paused a moment. "Whenever I mentioned my radio work everyone reacted like it was some kind of a hobby thing." She paused again, reflecting. "It is a risky business, and I wasn't confident enough about myself and my capabilities at graduation to even mention it as a career possibility." But after learning the retail business, Ellie also learned she had no passion for it. She began thinking more seriously about a radio career as she became more secure with herself.

"I know I'm good at management," she acknowledged and then added pragmatically, "I can always come back to it. Now I want to do what I have always felt, deep down inside, I should have done in the first place. I'm ready to try something risky, something adventurous, and I need to do it while I still have the guts to go for it."

Ellie was a realist. She recognized she had an uphill battle to convince someone to take a chance on a newcomer. ✻

As I begin to work on resumes with my clients, I notice they often stop with just a description of their previous job responsibilities. My advice is to carry that two steps further, telling the employer what skills you feel the experience required and what was the result of your having had the experience, what it accomplished. Noted career author Howard Figler points out you must make connections between what you have done in the past and what you can do in the future. Accomplishments can be either personal or professional. If you had a position in sales and you were named top volume winner for the year, say so. Skills and accomplishments can also be on a personal or volunteer level.

The job of editing will come later, but for now you should concentrate on getting familiar with all your experiences and dissecting them into responsibilities, skills and accomplishments. In the final resume, this section will change as your Career Objective changes, but for now you are developing a bank of experiences you will be able to rearrange as the need arises.

Write everything down so you can examine each activity in detail. One of the greatest benefits of getting your credentials down on paper is that it helps to pinpoint how they can be improved. In time you'll be able to pick each one of your activities apart in minute detail and describe in just a few short phrases the pertinent parts of each activity.

If you are changing fields entirely, the resume becomes one of your most important job search tools. It is your calling card, your first impression, your initial attempt to capture the attention of a prospective employer. It is a positioning statement; a profile of who you are and why you're qualified for the job you want; a concise means of introducing yourself to a potential employer. One way of looking at your resume is to think of it as a piece of direct mail advertising – and the product is you. As in any effective direct mail piece, it should be attractive in appearance, provocative in content, and positive in approach. The emphasis is always on what the product (you) has done and is capable of doing. Its purpose is to convince the employer you have enough of the necessary skills and experience to warrant an interview.

The next step is to organize the various elements that make for an effective resume and create a working draft. Start with the basic components. Since no two resumes should be the same, you should use the information you develop as you would an a la carte menu, choosing those that best suit the particular needs of each specific position. Look carefully at the information you've developed and choose the skills, interests and job related experiences that apply to this particular job. These are the only ones you'll want to incorporate into your resume.

I am always puzzled when people send out the same resume for a variety of positions and then are disappointed and even angry because no one responds. It is not uncommon for successful job changers to prepare four or five different resumes, all having basically the same information, but organized and presented differently for each Career Objective.

✸ *We went back over Ellie's radio experience. Throughout her college years Ellie had written copy, conducted interviews, and hosted an on-air talk show. We began to outline each of her jobs during the 10-15 hours a week she routinely spent as an intern at the station. We broke each of those positions down according to responsibilities, skills and accomplishments. As she began to get a better feel for her assets, she began to validate for herself that this change was truly the direction she wanted to go. This process encouraged her decision to make her move now and gave her the self-confidence she needed to meet the natural resistance she experienced from her family and friends who thought she had lost her mind.*

We reviewed her academic work, looking for lab classes that provided her with hands-on experience, with opportunities to translate theory into practice. "Don't overlook the significance of the research work you did for your senior thesis, or the work you did on your media images research project," I urged. All these experiences provided valuable skills and demonstrated experience in a variety of areas that she then translated into qualifications for the new job. ✸

For your first draft, start at the top of the page and list your name, address and telephone number, where it's easy for the employer to see. This information is not always as obvious as it seems.

Take your name for instance. Maybe you think this is only a cosmetic thing, but I believe what you call yourself and how others refer to you are very important in establishing the Professional Self you want to project. What you are trying to do is enhance that image. If you're thinking of a job at a bank, you'll want to present yourself as business-like, and William V. Smith, Jr., would be appropriate. If the job is in construction, Bill Smith will probably work just fine. And if you're looking at a job with a recreation department, Chip Smith makes you sound warm and friendly. Women looking for professional positions often find the use of initials helpful in overcoming gender bias. As you develop your own resume, ask yourself: Does the way I present my name match the company and the position I'm applying for?

✳ *Ellie looked at the job description she had brought from a small radio station in Santa Cruz, California. E. B. Fairchild had been the most appropriate signature for her management position. It was helpful in getting her ideas and recommendations reviewed in a neutral environment. In this case, however, she felt her nickname, Ellie, gave the right amount of informality for an on-air radio position.* ✳

Now think about your telephone number. Most personnel people prefer to work normal business hours. Especially when entry level positions are at stake, they are not likely to stay after five o'clock trying to reach you. Some research suggests the standard number of calls to a potential employee is three, then they give up and go on to the next on the list. If you have someone to take your messages during normal working hours, use that number. If you don't, I suggest an answering machine. Voice mail is becoming the norm. Personnel only has to call once to put the ball in your court.

Ambitious Professional Wants Good Title
Career Objectives

The next step is to develop a Career Objective. This is important as much for your sake as for your employer. Your Career Objective is your hypothesis. You are stating to the employer: "This is what I want to do." It gives your resume a focus. It also focuses you. With a clear objective, you can target your search towards a specific job market. It will also help you organize your entire job search into a coherent and manageable whole.

✻ *Ellie made her Career Objective specific: An entry level position with an easy listening radio station as an On-Air Personality providing an opportunity to utilize proven communication and organizational skills.*
We talked about the possibility of Ellie seeking technical work or management responsibilities at the radio station, areas where she unquestionably had credentials, but she was adamant — she wanted on-air experience and that was what she was going for.
"An on-air personality is anonymous," she explained, somewhat embarrassed. "I've always felt I've traded on my looks. It's important to me to be successful on my own, without people knowing what I look like." ✻

Your career objective can be flexible. Employers want to know that you want what they want. Under the best circumstances, a job description or position vacancy notice will give you a specific job title to list. This creates a framework for both you and the employer, and allows the option of selecting only those experiences that reflect your abilities in relation to that particular objective. Be specific about the kind of job you are looking for, or what skills you want to use, with what kind or type of organization, and, if it's important, where in the country.

Your career objective should give the employer some general career categories from which to evaluate the information on your resume. This is especially important if you are not responding to a specific position. Let's say, for example, a personnel director has two resumes in front of her, one without, one with a Career Objective. What is the personnel director supposed to do with the information on the first resume? Since the resume has not stated what the person is looking for, it's hard to evaluate whether or not the qualifications are appropriate.

The second resume states the person is looking for a position in Management. Immediately the personnel director can call to mind a current opening plus the skills or criteria she uses to evaluate a good manager. When she reviews the resume, she'll look for examples of organizational skills, communications skills, leadership positions, and budgeting experience. In short, she'll have enough information to evaluate your minimum qualifications for the position.

Be careful not to make your objective either the too general or too narrow. "Seeking a position which will utilize academic achievements and hands-on experience while providing for career development opportunities," could hardly help a job hunter's candidacy. On the other hand, "Seeking a management job in a health-care facility, with responsibility for programs, budget and staff supervision," could also work against you by eliminating you from other openings you might be equally qualified for.

Some of you may have to be more general, especially if you are blitzing several companies. "...an entry level position in sales," may be as close as you can come. In any case try to include:

- What you want to do (function).
- At what level (internship, entry level, trainee, middle-management, executive).
- In what setting (financial institution, aerospace industry, consumer products, retail, non-profit, government service).

For those who are still ambivalent about career objectives, Janice Weinberg, who operates a highly successful career consultation service in Westport, Connecticut, offers this solution in her book *How to Win the Job You Really Want*: "Move the objective from the resume onto the cover letter if your resume is transmitted by mail, or explain the objective in your initial discussion with the employer. This way, the employers get what they want, i.e., objectives tailored to their needs, and you get what you want: a resume that can be used in all instances."

The rest of the resume should now demonstrate the qualifications named in your Career Objective.

Experienced Administrator Has Done Everything
Skills, Experience and Accomplishments

Start with your experience. Remember that experience, as it appears on your resume, is anything you've done that allows you to confirm your ability to perform the functions of the job you are responding to. This includes actual paid full-time or part-time work, internships, volunteer work, and leadership positions in clubs and organizations.

For instance, the skills acquired as an inventory clerk might well translate into the skills necessary for billing in a doctor's or lawyer's office. A first grade teacher might translate her experience into adult education or training and development in the corporate world. A bank loan officer probably has the marketing and analytical skills required of a credit officer. A flight attendant might package himself as a customer service representative for a manufacturing company because taking care of people and their complaints is part of both jobs.

"Don't just say, 'I was responsible for this and responsible for that,'" advises Richard Fuchs, president of Karli & Associates, a Dallas-based outplacement and career counseling firm. "They don't want to hear what you were responsible for. Companies want to hear about results, what you accomplished."

"Show how, within the scope of your current job, your work made a difference. However minor the results may seem, a prospective employer likes to know you're aware that work should produce results – a job is more than simply performing the tasks in a job description.   Bottom-line results are especially important," advises career columnist Marilyn Moats Kennedy.   Most companies give little or no consideration to resumes that do not clearly point to the person's impact on company productivity – increased sales, reduced costs, improved output – anything that reflects positively on the bottom line.   What is it you may have to contribute that others may not?   You need to communicate that what you offer will truly add value to the organization.   Again I emphasize, be specific.   Rather than stating "top-producing, inventive engineer," try listing a few of the patents you received. Instead of just "Purchased all office equipment," a more powerful statement might say, "Researched and evaluated office equipment vendors for best prices and quality; negotiated all prices and terms."

✻ *We looked at Ellie's experience and how that supported her Career Objective. We started by reviewing the candidate specifications to determine where her strengths lay. Her retail experience covered her management skills well. Now she needed to think about how to present herself to the broadcasting world as an on-air personality.*

We began by determining what it takes to be a good radio personality. What kind of credentials and skills did Ellie already have that would convince someone that she could do this? She took a hard look at her volunteer work in college.   This led her into disk jockeying at weddings and special occasions through a free lance service operated by a friend, an activity she continued to pursue throughout her professional life as a manager. After some thought she listed three skills categories: radio, communications, and management.

In the first category, radio skills, she listed the tasks she had done at the university radio station during her four years there, including on-air interviewing, writing, research, reporting, and technical work.

She next looked at how she could transfer the skills she had acquired at her management position to the radio world. As a manager she had provided training and prepared reports for corporate meetings and conferences regarding her own department. This had sharpened her communications skills, her ability to get her point across in a clear and succinct manner in a way that was both enjoyable and informative. She felt this was important in presenting on-air information. She also believed it was necessary for a radio host to be able to fend off crises and remain calm when everything around her was falling apart.

"I remember one time in particular," she told me. "The entire fall line arrived just after several people were transferred out of my department. Before I had a chance to reorganize, the Chief Executive Officer blew in for his annual 'walk-through.'"

On the appointed day, she escorted the CEO through her department in a calm and professional manner, answering his questions and discussing future trends. He never suspected her whole department was in disarray at that exact moment. She summarized this as, "demonstrated ability to think and act under pressure."

She again drew on her retail experience to document her ability to meet deadlines. The third skill Ellie felt was important in determining on-air potential was leadership.

"You have to create a following of people who are interested in listening to you," she told me. "You have to attract people who want to hear what you have to say and value what your program offers them." So she looked to the leadership skills she developed in her management program. ✳

The major challenge in turning non-paid experience into a full-time job is to build sufficient credentials to make the new job seem a natural outgrowth of your previous experience rather than a radical departure. The realities of life are, however, that employers, and especially personnel departments, take a dim view of anything but paid work. You must clearly prove the significance of unpaid experience and how it relates to the job.

By taking the time to categorize each of your experiences into responsibilities, skills and accomplishments, you set up a primary data base from which a variety of resumes can come. In the future simply update your files, eliminating those items that are outdated or no longer pertinent and plugging in new information as necessary. This is equally true for chronological resumes.

This kind of preparation mentally catalogs all your qualifications for specific positions and helps prepare you for the interview. While you won't include everything on your resume, you'll have very specific examples to cite when the employer asks you to describe your ability to work under pressure, or to describe your management style. You'll be prepared for a multitude of questions because you are now aware of the breadth and depth of your experiences and how they relate to the job you want. If you can get all this onto a word processor you have an instant data base from which you can mix and match your entire array of information. Lacking this tool is no excuse for not developing individualized resumes, however, for herein lie the seeds for your success.

Next go back to your basic list. Determine where you meet or exceed the employer's requirements for the position. There are five specific areas you should explore:

- Education and Training
  List specific educational and training qualifications. Then develop a description of relevant experience that qualifies you to successfully meet these criteria.
- Knowledge
  Particularly look for the functional knowledge required by the position (marketing, sales, procurement, manufacturing, distribution, engineering, accounting, finance, personnel) to determine what specific qualifications are required.
- Experience
  Look at the range of the position (budgeting, strategic planning, number of functions to be managed, number of people to be managed). See what experience you have had in those areas.
- Personal Characteristics
  What personal characteristics are essential for good job performance in this position? Can you show you have these?
- Proficiencies

What certificates or licenses do you have? What computer programs are you proficient at?

A word of caution. Misrepresentation of job responsibilities has become perhaps the most substantial form of resume embellishment, and employers are leery of such dramatic action verbs as achieved, streamlined, managed, implemented. Many of these have been so abused they have become clichés and raise a flag to interviewers. As you develop your resume, be sure you can back up your claims with specific examples. Also beware of empty jargon such as "innovative, hands-on achiever" or "strong experience."

With this in mind, look at your skills. This is most often addressed by category in a functional style resume. This format is particularly useful for career changers, who want to move from one industry to another, or for someone who has held a series of non-related jobs. This works well in these instances because it showcases skill groupings, not where you acquired the skills.

Be specific about the kinds of expertise you want recognized by the person reviewing your resume. If, for example, you want a job in the advertising field, look for skills that prove your ability to produce material that increases sales or attendance, or creates media attention, and highlight these. Look for selling skills. If you used these or similar skills in three or four jobs, organize them by category. For example: Communication Skills, Sales Skills, Public Relations Skills, Artistic & Creative Skills. Under each of these major headings list your accomplishments that verify these skills. Don't mention the work site where you used them at this time, only the responsibilities and accomplishments. Focus on those things that are most important to the employer, those that the employer perceives to be important to the achievement of the organization's long-term strategic goals.

If your degree is recent enough, take a look at any of your course work that directly reflects your technical training and specialization. For example, if you have listed that you desire a position in management with computer companies and your degree is in Computer Science, it would be important to list additional course work you had that gave you the communication and people skills needed in management, such as psychology, financial accounting or debate. Don't list them all, five is a good average number.

✳ *Ellie listed drama, speech and psychology courses to add extra texture to her communications degree.* ✳

What Format is Best?
Functional vs. Traditional vs. Electronic

Be forewarned, functional resumes make many personnel directors uncomfortable. It's harder for them to figure out what you did where. They feel this approach is too involved for a resume and that this information is more appropriate for the interview. Others feel the format is used to hide something, such as a spotty record or limited work experience. To make this format effective, you must make it easy for the recruiter to understand.

Unless you have a really compelling reason, your best bet is still the standard chronological format, a job-by-job explanation of your work experience. It is especially effective for those with a steady progression of ever more responsible positions. In many instances the format alone will keep you in the applicant pool. Recruiters like it because it's faster to read and easier to assess.

If you go this route, list your work history in descending order by date. List under each employer the skills, experience and accomplishments that will be most valuable to your new employer, using the same techniques as in the functional format.

As we move towards the Twenty-First Century, and career search moves onto the Internet, a new form of resume is evolving, the electronic resume. Today forty percent of companies with more than 500 employees and all companies with 1,000 or more electronically scan resumes. There is good news and bad

news in this. As they say, first the good news. Electronic resumes have a longer shelf life, according the Jim Lemke, Manager, Employment and Human Resources Information Systems,
UCLA. Once the resume has been scanned it remains until specifically removed. The criteria for categorizing a resume are much
more specific and consistent relying on key words and job relationships, which means your resume has a higher probability to
getting seen by the right person. Electronic systems also file resumes under all appropriate categories, so if you don't fit the job
you applied for, you could be routed to something more suitable.
Scanning systems are color and gender blind.

On the other hand, to be effective, the electronic resume
must be able to communicate intelligently with the scanner. Most
work on some form of key word search. Be sure all your skills
are listed unambiguously. Be very specific. Don't say you are
computer literate. Say you have two years experience with an
IBM whatis, using UNIX, DOS, Windows or whatever. Don't
say "word processing," Say "experience with Word for Windows
6.0." List all of the programs you've ever worked with. List
whatever tools you've used. These translate to skills. Use dates,
the more recent the better.

Start with your most recent skills, as some scanning systems
only read the first eighty. Career columnist Joyce Lain Kennedy
suggests you start your resume with a skills paragraph – a paragraph made up of nothing but skill words. You then put these
words into context in the body of the resume.

"Read by itself, the key word paragraph doesn't make sense,
but it gets your attention," assures Lemke.

Other nitty-gritty advise he offers: Colors don't show up on
a scanner, so fancy paper is a waste. Make it standard letter size
paper. That's all the scanner reads. Laser print it if you can, or
use a typewriter or a bubble jet printer. A 24-pin dot matrix
printer will work, but don't use anything less than 300 dpi.

Don't fold or staple, mail it flat. If the paper is folded at a
crucial spot, the scanner may not pick out a key skill. Avoid

underlining as it can cut off the bottoms of letters and cause the scanner to misread it. Also avoid italics as they can also be misread. And if you were considering a two-column format, forget it. "It brings any system to its knees," Lemke says. Don't use smaller than 10-point type nor larger than 48-point.

If the company has an E-Mail address, send your resume this way, using ASCII format. You then know it's error free.

Your choice of resume format depends on what your previous experience has been and which will be the most effective sales piece for you. Some examples are given at the end of the chapter.

* As Ellie was obviously changing careers and a traditional resume would not support that change, she believed she had nothing to lose by using the functional style. *

Who You Worked For and How Long
Experience History

If you're using the functional format, you now list your experience so the potential employer will know where and for how long you used these skills. List only the positions that validate the skills section of your resume; eliminate non-significant positions. This is a straightforward list, giving the organization's name, location (city and state only), position(s) you held, and length of stay if longer than one year. Listing length of stay by months and years in specific blocks of time is a good idea, especially if you have a consistent work history.

There are some exceptions. For example, if you worked for the same organization every summer during college, rather than listing 6/87-9/87, 6/88-9/88, etc., it will be easier for the employer to grasp if you list length of employment as "4 consecutive summers."

A ten-year history of your experience is usually sufficient.

✳ In Ellie's case, she listed both her paid and unpaid positions under "Experience History." ✳

Enhancing Your Image
Selecting the Non-Essentials

Including professional affiliations, awards and honors or hobbies and interests is totally up to you. They provide additional texture to your resume, but they are not necessary ingredients. They aid in creating your desired image, but you may find that precious space could be put to better use in some of the more critical categories. If you decide to include one or all of these special sections, list only those that strengthen your resume or create some insight about the kind of person you are in terms of the company's goals.

Professional affiliations are the most obvious for inclusion. If you belong to professional organizations that benefit the employer, then by all means include them. Awards and honors give some understanding of the things you choose to excel in and the areas that you have been recognized for by other people. These are especially valuable if they have meaning to the company.

Hobbies and interests provide the employer with some clue as to how you define the quality of your life outside the working environment. It provides a general understanding of your personality, and how that fits with the organization's personality and that of the specific job. Mention a hobby only if you have demonstrable accomplishments in a field of serious endeavor or if your avocation suggests qualities that relate directly to job performance. As one of the functions of the resume is to create a certain amount of curiosity about who you are to trigger an interview, ask yourself: "Does this snap shot of me do this? What information shows me off best?"

Broadly educated people who can "piggy-back" their skills will find this section of the resume most valuable. For instance, listing fluency in a foreign language or computer expertise can be invaluable. "International experience" doesn't necessarily have to come from paid professional experience. Many employers also give weight to overseas living or study experience. If the job requires a high degree of eye-hand motor coordination, patience and concentration, you might mention leisure interests which also require these abilities (e.g., model airplane construction, crocheting, sewing) advises, Jo Danna, author of *Winning the Job Interview Game, Tips for the High-Tech Era*. Are you a person who enjoys competition and group activity such as participating in team sports? Are you quiet and reflective in your non-working hours, choosing to spend your time reading and involved in individual activities? Are you civic minded and involved in your community through volunteer work? Other examples of activities which involve occupational interests and abilities might be:

- Computer club
- Sketching, painting
- Writing short stories, poems
- Member of electronic bulletin board
- Repairing cars or small office equipment
- Little theater group (good for sales jobs)
- Toastmasters
- Rotary Club

It is important to list the professional licenses you have achieved or will need in order to do the work listed as your Career Objective. Many professions require board certification. If yours is one, make sure you list that information clearly on your resume. If you don't, more often than not the assumption is that you do not have it, and this could eliminate you from the applicant pool.

� *Ellie listed the broadcast license she had qualified for while in college and a demo tape she had made during one of her deejay sessions.* ✶

Beyond Degrees
Education

Next you'll want to list your education. As a matter of form, list your most advanced degree and/or your most recent degree first. For clarity's sake, employers want to know the name of the institution, the degree (bachelor of arts, master of science, etc.), major area of study, emphasis (if you had one in your major), and graduation date, if it is recent.

It is a matter of individual choice whether you list any other degrees or training you might have.

Do not omit your education because it is limited. Enlarge upon it where possible by listing company programs and home-study courses, for instance. This shows a desire for self-education readily understood by a sympathetic employer, who (like you) may not have had the opportunity for extensive formal education. The same employer will not be sympathetic to attempts at bluffing an education you do not have. The information you list in any section of your resume should first and foremost be truthful and reflect your qualifications for the kind of work you have listed as your Career Objective.

You should also include professional development opportunities outside a collegiate environment, such as on-the-job training programs or workshops and conferences you have attended that continue to advance your skill base.

✻ *Here's where Ellie listed her management training programs.*✻

Many career advisors believe employers assume references will be given when asked for and the ubiquitous sentence, "References provided upon request," is unnecessary. Your resume is just the first step in the marketing portion of your career search process. An employer will contact your references as one of the last things he does before making you a job offer. It's inappropriate to give information at the beginning of the process that will not be necessary until much later. You might want to keep a list of your references available during the interview portion of your job search in case you are asked for them at that time.

Putting It All Together
Effective Editing

Now it's time for the hard part: editing. The key to a good resume is brevity. Your resume should consist of short, well written, action statements, rather than complete sentences, that provide the employer with a well-rounded picture of your Professional Self, emphasizing the significant things that get your point across in a relatively brief space.

✴ *Now that all the material from her Personal Assessment had been organized, it was time for Ellie to refine it. Rustling through the papers, she looked dismayed.*
"But look at what you have to work with," I encouraged.
Ellie groaned. "You mean after writing down everything in the world, I need to leave most of it out? Thank God for word processors."✴

Whichever format you choose, it should take no more than two pages, with many employers preferring a one-page version. Remember most employers will skim through a resume to see if you meet minimum qualifications first. Make sure they can find them easily. Long and detailed resumes are often not given the attention they deserve because of time constraints.

If you are doing this on your own, you might want to get a second opinion about now. Have a career counselor or a friend read what you've done and ask them what message they get from it. Does it present your Professional Self as you have defined it? Refinements are easy at this point.

✴ *When Ellie returned the next week, she proudly placed the two-page resume on my desk.*

"Here it is. It's done." I reviewed it and agreed. Ellie's resume resulted in interviews with four small, out-of-state radio stations. All of the stations tried to push her into management, but she remained firm in her initial goal to be an on-air personality. She was finally offered a position at an easy-listening station in Reno, Nevada.

A year later she was promoted to program director for the station and was in that position for close to another year before she began to apply to larger radio stations in more significant markets with higher pay scales.

The last time I heard from Ellie she was a program director for a large radio station in the San Francisco area where she hoped to settle permanently. She had also taken on the additional risk of starting her own business: a special events disk jockeying service, employing several eager but inexperienced college students.

She believes she will eventually move away from programming and back into supervision because she knows she's good at it, and it will become a logical step. For now she's happy where she is, in a work environment she finds exciting and personally rewarding, and her salary now matches what she was making when she left her retail management position. *

The type of commitment you demonstrate in developing a well-thought-out resume is a good indicator of how serious you are about making a career change. If you are willing to dig deep enough to separate the appropriate elements of your Professional Self from all of life's experiences and present these in terms the company recognizes and appreciates, you'll be able to create the kind of resume that makes the employer want to know you better. To do that, they'll have to invite you for an interview.

Fuctional Resume Format

ELLIE FAIRCHILD
125 E. Oak Street
San Francisco, CA 94596
415-555-5151

CAREER OBJECTIVE
An entry level position with an easy listening radio station as an
On-Air Personality providing an opportunity to utilize proven com-
munication and organizational skills.

SIGNIFICANT SKILLS
Radio/Technical Skills
Four years of experience as an undergraduate working at a campus radio station. Responsibilities provided an opportunity to conduct on-air interviews on a variety of topics of interest to the campus
community, format musical sequences, program news breaks and provide technical assistance in the overall production and operation of a
24-hour station. Anchored a two-hour call-in program featuring comments from listening audience as well as music. Ratings remained
consistently high during the duration of the program.

Communication Skills
Throughout professional career have been responsible for the
preparation and presentation of departmental annual reports to Regional Manager. Effectively communicated budget and personnel
needs of department to supervisors resulting in increases in both areas. Performance appraisals over a three-year period consistently
ranked communication skills as superior. Have demonstrated ability
to think under pressure and put people at ease, while communicating
detailed information in an educational as well as entertaining manner.

Management Skills
Successfully managed Handbag and Accessories Department
for a national department store located in the Bay Area. Responsible
for all aspects of personnel, budget and sales for a department with

annual sales of $250,000. Was promoted to department manager after completion of sales promotion which increased sales by 15% over a two month period. Demonstrated strong commitment to team approach and welcomed comments from staff regarding management style.

EXPERIENCE HISTORY

KCSB Radio Station, University of California, Santa Barbara, 4 years
Macy's Department Store, San Francisco, CA, 3 years
Travelling Melodies DeeJay Services, San Francisco CA, 2 years

EDUCATION & TRAINING

University of California, Santa Barbara
Bachelor of Arts, Communication Studies, June 1984
Macy's Department Store Executive Training Program, San Francisco, CA (1-year program)

Significant Course Work:

Fundamentals of Acting
Voice Laboratory
Social Aspects of Behavior
Human Information Processing
Principles of Communication and Language
Public Speaking

AWARDS & HONORS

American Association of University Women, Undergraduate Scholarship Recipient, 2 consecutive years
Macy's Circle of Excellence Award, 1986
Girls Clubs of America, Certificate of Appreciation for Outstanding Volunteer Service, 1985

HOBBIES & INTERESTS:

Competitive running and cycling, coaching girls tennis and writing short stories

References and audition tape available upon request

Traditional Chronological Resume Format

Alice Palmer

425 Meigs Road   Santa Barbara, CA 93101
(805) 555-7688

OBJECTIVE

To obtain an entry-level assistant account executive position that utilizes my communication skills and creative abilities.

EXPERIENCE

Design Intern. Santa Barbara *Independent*, March 1988 to Present. Create and design visual presentation of print advertising in weekly entertainment newspaper. Demonstrate ability to work under pressure and meet deadlines while developing quick and precise paste-up, layout, and type-spec'ing skills. Assist with weekly production of editorial layout. Work closely with advertising client representatives in interpretation and execution of advertising concepts.

Marketing Assistant. International Transducer Corporation, August 1986 to March 1988.
Exhibited strong verbal and written skills in customer service capacity. Accountability and organization required in maintaining quotation records for accurate sales projections. Served as foreign sales representatives' liaison. Responsible for distribution of product literature and compilation of customer and competitor information files. Organized and executed ITC's participation in undersea technology trade show. Position required flexible interpersonal skills to interact with multi-level positions.

Fundraiser: Charitable Funding Group, July 1986 to August 1986. Raised $2,500 in one-month period from community members for construction of park facility. Sensitivity and tact were imperative to encourage donations for memorial site construction from families of Vietnam veterans. Adapted and composed caller script which was adopted as official script.

Office Manager: UCSB Student Government Office, January 1985 to June 1986.
Supervisory and leadership abilities highlighted in the management of a five-person clerical staff. Formulated and maintained $35,000 operating budget. Communication skills emphasized in meeting participation. Oriented new student officers to office policies/procedures and equipment operation. Promoted professional relationship between student officers and permanent career staff members.

Fundraiser: UCSB Annual Fund Program, October 1984 to January 1985.
Negotiated over $10,500 in pledges from UCSB parents and alumni. Recognized as top caller with a cumulative 47% pledge rate and an average gift of $102. Wide knowledge of campus programs proved beneficial. Initiative and persistent attitude were necessary to meet target goals.

EDUCATION

B.A., Communication Studies, July 1988
University of California, Santa Barbara

Additional Coursework
Santa Barbara Community College
    Introduction to Advertising
    Introduction to Graphic Design
    Introduction to Pagemaker

ACTIVITIES

Associated Students Advertising & Publicity Board, September 1984 to June 1986
Fulfilled positions of Newsletter Editor, Treasurer and Fundraising Organizer.

UCSB Advertising Club, 1983 to 1984
As a member, participated in development of award winning campaign for collegiate competition.

REFERENCES
Available upon request

Electronic Resume Format

JOHN S. FRANKLIN, CPE
1321 Greeley Street
Sudbury, MA 01776
(508) 443-5555

OBJECTIVES: Corporate Management
A highly capable manager of facilities operations and maintenance, occupancy services, space planning, capital forecasting and justification, budgeting and control, workload planning and directing support activities in both aerospace and commercial industries.

KEY WORDS:
Certified Plant Engineer, space planning, engineering, new construction, lease negotiation, maintenance, communications services, energy conservation, environmental programs, government interface, budget forecasting, capital planning, occupancy services, A&E contracts, standards development, budget preparation, personnel training, performance scheduling, administrative control, technical direction, management of CPFF, T&M and FP contracts, workload planning, occupancy services, capital forecasting and justification, budgeting and control, CMMS, MS Office and PM5.

CAREER HISTORY
Raytheon Company, Goleta, California   1980-1995
Manager, Plant Engineering and Facilities
    Responsible for managing the division's $300M investment in facilities, space and utilities, providing space planning, engineering, new construction, lease negotiation, modernization of existing facilities (including clean rooms), maintenance and communications services for the research, development, engineering and manufacturing of electronic systems. Directed energy conservation, safety and environmental programs, including hazardous waste generation and disposal, providing the interface for Federal, State and local agencies, $11M budget development and oversight.

Polaroid Corporation, Cambridge, Massachusetts   1967-1980
Manager, Engineering and Occupancy
   Provided management for the Cambridge properties including space planning and forecasting, leasehold evaluation, capital planning and occupancy services. Supervised A&E contracts, development of standards, budget preparation and personnel training for Corporate Facilities organization.

Sylvania Electronic Systems, Waltham, Massachusetts 1962-1967
Project Engineer
   Developed facilities criteria and space planning for construction of buildings, utilities and site for radar/missile facilities. Included performance scheduling, change order and design criteria. Provided administrative and technical direction to field installation teams.

GD/Astronautics, San Diego, California   1959-1962
Installation Support Supervisor
   Provided administrative control and technical direction of subcontractors for the activation of Atlas missile complexes. Included management of CPFF, T&M, and FP contracts for installation, maintenance, validation and spares provisioning for facilities and Ground Support Equipment.

TWA, Kansas City, Missouri   1958-1959
Senior Facilities Engineer
   Prepared designs for commercial jet aircraft facilities nationwide.

General Motors Corporation, Kansas City, Kansas   1955-1958
Facilities Engineer
   Prepared designs for automotive production facilities.

EDUCATION:
   MS Engineering Management — Northeastern University
   BS Mechanical Engineering — GMI

9 Interviewing With Confidence
Creating a job-winning image

> *"The person who gets the job offer is not always the most qualified, but rather the one best able to articulate their qualifications for the job."*

A s you are keenly aware, the interview is now-or-never time. You can't afford to blow it, so make sure you're good at it. This is your job. As you work at it, you'll get better. Recognize it for what it is, performance art. You don't have to enjoy it, but you do have to do it well.

Most people judge you by the way you value yourself. You must display poise and self-assurance; you must project the impression that you have the utmost confidence in your ability to do an outstanding job in this new position. If you don't come across as confident, how can you expect the employer to feel confident in hiring you? Act timidly and people will think of you as timid.

   ✳ *Madeline Aguirre now commands a comfortable corner office in a multi-storied building in downtown Los Angeles, with a sign on the door stating "Director of Corporate Training." A far cry from the day four years earlier that a shy, retiring, 32-year-old Hispanic woman sat across from me, looking for an accounting position. She appeared to shrink into her chair. When asked to talk about herself, the words came out one by one, as if physically forced. She squirmed in her seat when asked to describe her accomplishments. When I pressed her to be more expansive, she blushed and told me how her parents had always taught her "it wasn't nice" to be "boastful," to "brag" about one's accomplishments. More than that, she wasn't sure she had much to boast about.*

But she was here with a purpose.

"I've been asked to come in for an interview," she said, then hesitated. "Too many times I've come away from the interview with nothing. I know I lose it right there, and to people I know are no more qualified than I." Here a spark of rage took hold. Her dark eyes snapped while her fist clenched, ready to pound out her frustration on the chair arm. Here was a determined lady. I asked for some background.

During her high school and college years, Madeline had helped out in the family business, a Mexican restaurant in the Greater Los Angeles area. As expected of a good daughter, she had done whatever was necessary. She waited tables, she ordered food, filled water glasses, and cooked. Later she took over the bookkeeping, filled out the required government forms, and ordered food supplies.

While at college, where she earned her BS in accounting, most of her classmates took advantage of school sponsored internship programs, but Madeline had no time left for these. During campus recruiting interviews, when the prestigious Big Six accounting firms asked about her work experience, she simply hung her head shyly, much like she did before me now, and said she had none. This cost her dearly. Most of her interview feedback acknowledged she had the necessary technical skills and experience, but the jobs also required someone who would be aggressive in generating clients and assertive in her dealings with them. In this she failed. Her technical skills came wrapped in a timid, diffident demeanor. She didn't seem as if she could do the job.

Although recruiters often pointed this out to her, she didn't understand what they meant and could never put this criticism into a useful perspective. Unable to acknowledge her real problem, but armed with her accounting degree, she continued to apply for professional positions, but with no better luck. She finally settled for a bookkeeping job, a position that did not require, nor pay for, her knowledge of accounting, a sore disappointment after her years of preparation. She was underemployed, undervalued, and her future prospects were bleak. Madeline wondered if she did indeed have the skills necessary for a more responsible job. Otherwise, why had she not landed one?

The first job turned out to be as disappointing as the salary, and before long she moved on to another. She continued to accept a series of paraprofessional positions from employers who maintained that if she accepted these lower positions and did the professional work, when a position that she was qualified for in the professional ranks became available, they would consider her. She tried to be patient and optimistic.

Fate stepped in at this point and dealt her another hard blow. Her mother became seriously ill and forcing her to leave her job, come back home and help in the family restaurant again.

I looked at her resume. I understood why employers saw her as a professional risk. Besides the interruption to help out in the family crisis, she had held none of her jobs for any sustained period of time and I asked her why.

"I've never been given what I was promised. Sure, I've gotten good evaluations, but I've never been promoted. They were all the same, and all the work so boring. I left each job hoping the next one would be better." Her eyes began snapping again. "When it happened this last time, I knew I had to do something." This time the fist came down solidly on the chair.

"First my new supervisor was hired at twice my salary. Then she couldn't do the job and when they found out, I was asked to train her! But that's not the half of it. When they finally fired her because of incompetence, the department head asked me to fill in until a qualified person could be found. I told him I wanted to be considered for the position, and gave him my resume. He told me it was unusual for the organization to move someone from the support ranks to the professional ranks. It just was not done, and I would need a lot more experience. When I pointed out I had a bachelor's degree in accounting he told me that I hadn't used my accounting since graduation and was too rusty for the job. My degree was no longer an asset and my performance on the job counted for nothing. I quit that very day."

She went back to the restaurant business as an interim step while she continued her search for work in her chosen field.

She sent out resumes in response to several ads for accountants and one of the companies finally asked her to come in for an interview. She passed the ad across my desk.

"I know I can do this job, but too many times, after the interview, I never hear from them again. I'm tired of that. Can you help me?" ✱

According to a study by Northwestern University of 405 top employers, the number one reason for an applicant not getting the job is poor personality and manner; followed by lack of poise, poor presentation of self, lack of confidence, and a timid, hesitant approach.

Applying for a new job often becomes a matter of persuading yourself that you're not stepping out of your league, that you're not misrepresenting yourself, that you're not faking it. Sometimes it feels like an act, but once you present yourself this way, people accept you as a self-assured person, and because people treat you as a confident, valuable person, a new Professional Self emerges. You become that new self.

The one central question in all interviews that often remains unspoken is, "Why should I hire you?" If you think of the interviewer as having this central objective in mind rather than simply scrutinizing you or picking you apart, you will interview more comfortably and effectively. Just keep "Why should *I* be hired?" in mind and design every one of your responses so that it gives the employer another reason for choosing you. One common reason for nervousness going into a job interview is fear you won't get an offer. Just tell yourself that if you don't get an offer, you're no worse off than before.

I call the interview the "two head test." You can assume the organization sees you as at least minimally qualified since you made it to the interview stage. Now they want to see what you look like and how you operate in a stressful situation. This is where they evaluate your personality style and your personal strengths and abilities. That's why it's so important to be well prepared.

> **Remember that although the interviewer controls the
> flow of the interview, you control its content.**

You are responsible for making the interview interesting and informative. Keep in mind the interview is *your* opportunity to let the employer know you understand that while others are also qualified, you are the *best* candidate because you bring assets to the organization that are uniquely your own. By hiring you, the organization will benefit from all the other skills and abilities you have mastered and gathered during your lifetime. Focus on those things the employer perceives to be important to the achievement of the organization's long-term strategic goals. The more the interviewer perceives you as possessing these capabilities, the greater your chances of getting an offer.

    ✳ *We put the ad Madeline had answered in front of us, and broke it down into individual skills. We culled from her experience and skills those that fit the specifics of the job in front of us, much as Pat did in Chapter 3.*

    Next we addressed her work history. She retreated again. "My present employment is at the restaurant," she reminded me.

    I asked her to tell me exactly what she did there.

    Slowly she began to recount her current responsibilities. "I hire the staff. I train the new employees," she began. It turned out she also ordered all food and supplies, and was, in fact, the financial officer and chief accountant for the organization. Her books were regularly audited, and each time she received compliments on their completeness and accuracy. She had obviously put her accounting background to good use.

    Next we delved into her volunteer work, the clubs and organizations she belonged to, her travel experiences.

    "Let's see. After the Guatemalan earthquake, I helped organize food supplies to be sent to refugees. As a matter of fact, I was between jobs just then, so I went there and stayed for six months training other volunteers. My Spanish came in handy."

    After further review, we added computer and writing skills to her list. ✳

    You must describe your skills in concise, unambiguous terms; back up your claims by referring to actual experiences in your life; and make a clear connection between your skills and the needs of the employer.

    There are two parts to every interview:

- You must convince the company you have the necessary experience and skills to do the job.

● You must persuade the interviewer your unique life experiences will benefit the organization.

The extras you provide will make a difference when the employer decides who is the "most" qualified. The employer sees this as the candidate who will make the biggest contribution above and beyond the specifics of the job.

Creating the Sizzle
Establishing Your Experience and Skills

Your first step is to identify what you gained from your experiences and how that applies to the position at hand. You need to carefully think about the conceptual similarities that exist between this job and the other jobs you've held. That way, when you hear an objection about the differences between your experience and the company's requirements, you can counter with the similarities. Then give examples to support this. In sales this is called "overcoming objections."

Look for ways to "piggy-back" your skills. People who can do this will not only be the most marketable, but also the most promotable and the highest paid, according to Maxine Wineapple, president of New Options Programs, a career counseling service. As an example, a degree in computer science will open many doors in the nineties, but a fluency in Japanese increases the computer scientist's opportunities dramatically. Add to that management expertise, and the Japanese-speaking computer scientist is virtually assured entree into a fast-track career, she points out.

＊ *Madeline made notes, organizing around the specific skills and experiences required for this particular job. She looked for where she had developed these skills and experiences and how she used them in particular tasks. She needed to learn not to trivialize her assets, but to imagine contexts where they would be useful. The quieter you keep about your strengths, the more easily they tend to fade into the wood-work and become invisible even to yourself, as Madeline had found.* ✱

Selling What You Will Do For The Company
Adding Value to Your Candidacy

The next step is selling the company on what you can do for it. Begin by studying the company itself.

The shortest interview I ever witnessed was at a west coast university.

Motorola was interviewing graduating seniors for entry level positions. Adam, a very qualified student, entered the interview room only to emerge a scant two minutes later, ashen faced, astonished and dismayed. Once he recovered from the shock, he told me the first thing the interviewer asked was what he knew about the company. Adam began by saying what great televisions Motorola made and how his family had purchased them for years.

The interviewer asked Adam if he had read the information the company had sent to the campus recruiting office on this particular Motorola division. Surprised, he responded he had not, but he planned to do so as soon as the interview was over.

The interviewer stood up and shook his hand, said the interview was over and showed him the door. If Adam had done his homework, he would have learned this particular division of Motorola was the Satellite Division and had no connection at all with TV's.

Employers expect you to know what you are interviewing for, what the organization's products and services are, who they serve, their location, and other pertinent information regarding the organization and to incorporate that information into your answers during the interview.

✱ *I outlined the steps in Chapter 6 on research, and Madeline went to work.*

*She returned the next week, notes in hand. She had learned from the company's annual report that it had recently purchased a business that provides meals for four major airlines. She was excited to see how she could relate her accounting degree, her restaurant experience, and her other volunteer experience to the organization.**

The interviewer may try to find out how well you have prepared by asking you to comment on your own career path within the company. Think about this carefully in terms of the goals of the organization, so the interviewer will know your career goals are realistic within the organization's structure, and that this position is a logical step.

Even if not asked directly, having this information at hand enhances your own comfort level. You can also use this information effectively at the end of the interview, when asked, "Do you have any questions?"

You might also find an organization chart helpful, and a call to the company will often get this for you. Ask for the Industrial Relations, Personnel or Public Affairs Department. Ask for a job description. Besides being helpful to you, this indicates the level of your interest in the position. If they are unwilling to send you information, see if the person who contacts you for the interview will discuss these items with you.

There are other ways of getting information. For instance, if a placement agency has arranged your interview, you can probe your counselor about the position. Try to find out as much as you can about the person who is conducting the interview, including whether this will be a screening or a selection interview. If she's not too busy when you arrive, ask the secretary or receptionist friendly questions about the organization. Browse through any company literature you find there.

Interviewers are always trying to fill specific positions. There will be certain characteristics they will be looking for, including your past performance, as they believe this to be the single best predictor of success in the future. Prepare examples of times you've used a variety of skills in situations that are similar to the ones listed in the job description. When the interviewer asks, "How would you handle..." or "Give me an example of..." they are looking for clues to how you process information, develop solutions, or tackle problems. Don't concern yourself so much with whether the answer is right, but rather focus on the process by which you arrived at the solution and be prepared to provide detail about that process. Back up your statements with examples, illustrations, descriptions, statistics, comparisons or testimonials. This helps clarify your comments, helps to substantiate them, helps the listener remember them, and adds interest to your presentation. Always, always affirm the positive and sound confident.

"No boss will pay you to prove that you can do something you haven't already done. First he wants to see you solve the problems he hired you to solve," says New York management consultant Martin Yate, author of *Knock 'em Dead: With Great Answers to Interview Questions.* The closer your research determines what these particulars are and how you have used them, the more qualified you appear.

On the other hand, don't worry if you haven't done everything. As a general guideline I like to use what I call the 50-30-20 rule. You should be one hundred percent proficient at fifty percent of job. You should be able to become proficient in thirty percent of the job in three to six months given proper training and orientation. And twenty percent of the job should be totally new to you.

If you are one hundred percent qualified the day you walk into the job, you are also overqualified and underpaid from that day on. Having half the job in the bag is your assurance to the employer they are getting their money's worth. The next thirty percent is the employer's commitment to you as a working professional. The last twenty percent is your commitment to yourself to continue your own growth and increase your skill bank with each new position.

✳ *I asked Madeline to think back on the work we had done and to determine how she might truly add value to this employer's organization.*

Madeline's responsibility during the interview was to demonstrate both verbally and by her presence this uniqueness and individuality. Professional recruiters often complain that candidates are not verbal enough and do not give concrete examples of their experience and how it pertains to their professional potential. This had certainly been true of Madeline. ✳

Don't be reluctant to talk about yourself and your accomplishments. Remember, the interviewer wants to know more about you, especially your potential value to the organization. The more information you can communicate, the stronger your position will be.

As you prepare for you interview, testing out your strategy can significantly improve your chances of success. Now is a good time to arrange for a mock interview with a career counselor, or at least a good objective friend. It will help to clarify your presentation both in style and content. It's hard for you to see the big picture when you're standing in the frame.

Stacking the Deck in Your Favor
Selling Yourself

It all comes down to the 45 minutes you spend face to face with the interviewer. In study after study employers say the job interview is the single most important activity in determining whom they hire.

John L. Lafevre, in his book, *A Peek Inside the Recruiter's Briefcase,* describes interviewers as "merely professional gamblers who have been provided a 30-minute tip sheet analysis to help them decide on which candidate to place the bet." In fact most decisions are made on visceral reactions to interviewees by the person making the decision. And quite possibly the decision will be made by the time you sit down. Your basic objective is to spark a positive feeling from the time you step into the office.

The interviewer wants to confirm this spot decision.   He wants to know who you are as a person, as an individual with a certain amount of uniqueness. This is your chance to show your stuff, the place where your motivations and the employer's needs come together.

That's not always easy. People from other cultural backgrounds often have their confidence eroded by negotiating in a different society.   One of the factors often facing first generation college graduates, many of whom are minorities and women, is that no one has gone before them who can tell them what it's like.

"People may know very little about the communication system of Blacks or Asians," according to management consultant, Onolee Zwicke, who points out that some cultures are traditionally demonstrative, while others are more restrained. If their culture has socialized them to be non-assertive by Western standards, they may have learned to be modest, self-effacing, reserved, quiet or dependent on others. Self-deprecation becomes a ritual way of getting information out without appearing to boast; but interviewers often take this modest demeanor as a genuine lack of self-confidence. For these reasons women and people of color may find it especially challenging to be forthright about their own strengths and achievements. But you must get straight with yourself that you have something to offer, and you must be willing to say it to anyone who needs to hear it.

   ✸ *No one in Madeline's family had interviewed for a professional situation. She had no idea of the kind of information that needed to be shared and did not know how to prepare. As a result, she walked into an interview feeling terrorized by her ignorance and too intimidated to express herself well. Simply put, good interviewing is good salesmanship. The people she lost to were just better able to sell themselves.* ✸

It is not outrageous to say in an interview, "I know I can do the job you want done, and I have plenty of examples to back up what I'm saying." That isn't cocky. It's an honest expression of your belief in yourself, regardless of what the other candidates may have in their backgrounds.

Interviewing for a job is a truly American practice, and until recently, one dominated by white males. Other country's employment traditions appear strange to Americans who are often unsuccessful in their initial interviews abroad because they rely on how it's done here at home.

What we're talking about are the tools for survival in the American marketplace. One of the basic skills for success is interviewing well. It is as basic as learning to write. By injecting your own personality into the interview you let the employer know that you value yourself as a person, you like who you are and believe that, in addition to your professional qualifications, you have many other qualities to offer the employer who is lucky enough to hire you.

* *Body language was especially important in Madeline's case. She was quite small in stature, and when she compressed herself into her chair, she appeared frail and birdlike. We began with a difficult discussion on how she could project the necessary confidence. Being an Hispanic woman myself, I pointed out how we use our hands when we speak, and how these gestures are a part of our communication style. Madeline agreed, and yet, before me now, she sat quietly, her hands under careful control. She felt the natural effervescence she displayed in social situations was inappropriate in the workplace. "It's appropriate if used in a way that exhibits your comfort level with yourself," I told her.*

I assured Madeline that it was not necessary to jeopardize her cultural background or to assume she had to adopt this style in other areas of her life.

Next I asked her to describe herself, what she brought to the table. Here she smacked solidly into a mental wall, finding nothing to say beyond her resume, again a common reaction. *

To help my clients understand their own personal skills and abilities, I begin by asking how three of their best friends would describe them. Describing themselves in the third person feels more comfortable at first and with practice they are soon able to articulate their distinctiveness and not feel uncomfortably boastful.

Here are some questions I ask to get them started:

● Are you the person in your group that always balances the check after dinner, determining how much everybody pays?
● Are you the one that can organize a party on a moment's notice, complete with hats and horns?
● Do people come to you as a sounding board when they need some clarity on a problem they are having?
● Are you artistic?
● Just what is it that your friends value in you? What skills do these suggest?

For instance, the compulsive person who does everything in the same order according to schedule, is also the person who keeps perfect and orderly records of all calls, correspondence, and visitors. The confrontational person who can't help being very direct with people, is the same person who can approach customers who are behind in their payments. Note if you have a well-developed sense of humor, you are very organized, you put people at ease, you are creative, and begin to develop a plan for incorporating those strengths into your professional profile.

It also helps to start letting your friends know when you've done something that makes you proud. Tell them when you've had a success. Call your family when you've accomplished something that makes you proud. Tell your boss or coworkers about projects you've completed or problems you've solved. While you may feel uncomfortable talking about yourself at first, keep in mind that, as with anything else, you improve with practice. It gets easier as your confidence builds and it is confidence that separates the successful from the also-rans.

> *Self-confidence is based on an honest, unabashed comfort with your skills and abilities.*

Self-confidence manifests itself in your behavior. Even if this is difficult, if you make the interviewer think you believe in yourself, you'll be on the right track.

If a lack of confidence is persistent and you cannot seem to rid yourself of these feelings no matter what you do, you might want to explore where your feelings come from with a counselor. General feelings of low self-esteem will continually hamper your job search if you leave them unattended.

Inevitably, during the course of the interviewing process you will see other candidates who will impress you and you'll imagine you don't have a chance. Don't assume yourself into a position where style rather than essence intimidates you. The person who gets the job offer is not necessarily the most qualified, but rather the one best able to articulate their qualifications. Your job is to make sure that person is you.

Putting Yourself in Control
Basic Preparation

Break down everything you've learned about yourself and about the company so far into the five major areas the interviewer will want to get at:

- Educational history.
- Work and experience.
- Personal skills and attributes.
- Career and professional goals.
- Knowledge of the organization.

File all your information under these five categories. When asked a question, you'll be able to determine quickly which of the five mental files to access.

An important goal of any job interview should be to obtain useful information to determine whether the job is right for you. Is this a "good fit?" Is the "corporate culture" one you understand and can function with? Success in the interview may mean learning that the position is not for you. If you see your goal as gathering information, you're more likely to perform better. This is not a win-lose game, but an exchange of useful information between you both. Level the playing field by giving the employer the information they need to hear from you in an orderly, confident and interesting manner. Your use of examples and anecdotal information will showcase your skills and qualifications within the framework of a story.

In order to make the interview a relaxed, mutual exchange of information, you must have a flexible agenda of the points you want to raise. This helps you maintain control. That control, whether real or psychological, can go a long way in maintaining your composure during the initial interview and in subsequent meetings. Now is the time to query the interviewer on how he views the position and the tasks he wants accomplished. Get this information as early in the interview as possible so that you can tailor your experience and skills to the needs he reveals.

You must be comfortable in the interview setting in order to make the best impression. One good way to do this is to know in advance how you'll respond to a variety of questions an interviewer might pose. There are a number of commonly asked questions you can anticipate. For instance, interviewers may probe your decision-making approaches with questions such as:

"I'm curious to know what you would do if..."
"What were your three most important responsibilities in that job?"

"What special skills or knowledge did you need to perform these duties?"

Other common questions, especially if your job experience is limited, are:

"What do you see as your best quality? Your worst?"
"What was your most difficult class in college and what did you learn from it?"
"Which one of your skills do you think you will use most in this position and why?"

(A list of fifty most commonly asked questions will be found at the end of this chapter.)

These questions generally reduce to one of three varieties:

Why us? Why have you chosen to apply here? What interests you about our organization?
Why you? Why should we be especially interested in you over others?
Why now? What makes this the right time for you and us?

While I don't suggest memorizing a series of answers that will sound stiff and unnatural, I do encourage you to develop an outline of areas you would like to cover in your interview and come up with ideas on how to respond if asked these questions. Practice your responses so that you present your qualifications and individuality well. Do this enough times before the interview so they sound comfortable coming out of your mouth, like you are talking about someone you know very well, not someone you've just met. Your interviewing style showcases the information from the personal data base you presented on your resume and any other information you feel is appropriate to the position.

I must emphasize how important it is to practice your answers out loud. One method I find to be exceptionally helpful is to use a tape recorder and then play the answers back for review. How do you sound? Are there a lot of pauses, "ahems" and "you know's" in your answers? Ask yourself, if you were in the interviewer's position, would you hire the person on the tape? Repeating your answers three or four times, or having someone else critique them, will generate a certain amount of comfort on your part and improve the quality of your responses.

＊ *Madeline returned the next week looking composed and confident.*

"I can't tell you how uncomfortable it was to practice out loud," *she confessed after her first attempt with the tape recorder. She* *stumbled on nearly all of the sample questions.*

"My mind either drew an immediate blank, or I rambled on and on. Sometimes I just spouted nonsense." But she stuck to it, thought each question through, and tried again. Her goal was to paint a verbal picture of herself as someone capable of performing the functions and responsibilities cited in the job description. She confronted herself in front of a mirror, and when she was confident with that, she gave the list of questions to her roommate and asked her to pick ten random questions. When she was comfortable with this, she went back to the mirror for more polish with those she felt were the most important. ＊

As I said before, examples are important and demonstrate that you have prepared and given the interview some thought before hand. Go through a series of practice interviews. If you are not working with a career counselor, enlist the help of a neighbor, a friend, or a significant other; someone who can offer an unbiased opinion of your interview style.

Identify three anecdotes or examples that illustrate your qualifications for the job, stories that tell of your uncovering specific issues while conducting research for the interview, reviews of past experiences, sincere expressions of motivations, or interesting examples of your most significant accomplishments. Practice your answers while you are dressing in the morning. Look at yourself in the mirror. Do you look relaxed? Can you meet your own gaze in the mirror? Will you be able to look directly at the interviewer? With practice these things become naturally incorporated into your repertoire of responses.

The final preparation is for the last two commonly asked questions: "Is there anything you'd like to add?" and "Do you have any questions to ask me?"

In response to "Is there anything you'd like to add?" always restate your interest in the position and underscore your qualifications or skills. If the interviewer failed to ask questions that allowed you to talk about your chief qualities, bring them up now. Be sure to reread your resume before the interview to remind yourself of the key points you want to get across.

Your response to "Do you have any questions to ask me?" depends upon what has previously occurred. Ideally, you will have already familiarized yourself with the occupational field in general and the interviewing organization in particular. Then, you will have framed some questions that are of critical importance to you in line with your career goals. Be sure you cover them. Some questions you might want to consider are:

"What created the job opening?"
"How will my performance be measured?"
"May I see a job description?"
"May I see an organization chart?"

✴ *Confidence problems can be dealt with and improved, as Madeline demonstrated as we practiced together. She soon found her nervousness and discomfort level easing. She began to list what made her different: her bilingual abilities, the tact and diplomacy she had learned from years in the restaurant business, the ability to stick to a task until completion.*

"I'll never remember it all," Madeline lamented, shuffling through her research. "I know I'll forget something important." ✴

If you have to, put your final questions on small file cards. Look them over to see that everything has been addressed. By developing questions prior to the interview, you demonstrate concern about the position as well as preparation for the interview. Most interviewers will view you in a positive manner if you do this. Questions about the business side of the firm are also valuable as they not only mark you as a serious, ambitious candidate with a definite future. If your interviewer gives embarrassed or evasive answers to any of the questions, you can be sure there is something to be embarrassed or evasive about.

If the interview was very thorough, the only question might be "When can I expect to hear from you?"

If you are asked back for a second interview, you'll prepare essentially the same as for the first. Most likely this will be with a different person, so all your initial information will be new.

You might want to review your first interview. Here is the perfect opportunity to use 20/20 hindsight. What could you have done better? What did you forget that you wished you had said? What good examples have you just remembered? What were the really strong points you want to reemphasize?

Whether it is a screening interview or a selection interview, you should know who is to make the next move, and what that move is to be. Do you need to furnish more information – a transcript, a completed application, references, an example of your work? Will the employer get in touch with you, or you with him or her? Approximately when?

In addition, if the interview was for selection purposes, you should know the duties of the position, the supervisory structure, the employer's expectations of you, the working environment, the reason for the opening (newly created, resignation, promotion, reorganization, or the company's expansion into a new market), the salary range and benefits. This is usually the time references are brought up.

My Biggest Fans
References

Choose people who can speak to your qualifications for this particular job. Make sure you've talked to them about the kind of employment you're looking for and why you think they can speak to your qualifications. Give them a copy of your resume and any pertinent information that will make their recommendation stronger and more personal.

Professional recruiters are always able to spot references that have had only minimal contact with the perspective employee and conversely are able to spot those that know them well. Follow up with your references regarding the status of your job search and make sure to send the appropriate thank you notes once you've gotten the job. This kind of follow up ensures a good, professional memory for your references and enhances your chances of using them in the future.

The Time, the Place, and Looking the Part
Nitty-Gritty Common Sense

It is important that you be on time. Punctuality is essential. If you are scheduled for an on-site interview, it is a good idea to call ahead and ask where you should park, what office you need to report to, how long the interview will be. This is particularly important if you are interviewing in another city or with a large organization where you might have to pass through a security clearance.

If you know in advance what to expect, there should be no surprises that may cause you to be late or miss the interview entirely, such as one applicant who missed a tricky freeway exit. She was 15 minutes late for the meeting. The interviewer informed her he had allowed her 30 minutes to make her case, and she had already used up half of that. I know of another instance where the company name was not on the building.

Appropriate dress is very important. If you want to be taken seriously as a professional, you must look like a professional. For both men and women, a suit is a must. More often than not, you will dress more formally for the interview than you will for the job. This was true for one man who was applying for a position where he would wear coveralls. He impressed the employer when he appeared for the interview in his only suit and he got the job.

✱ *Madeline did not trust her own fashion sense. Her wardrobe was heavily weighted towards the casual and comfortable. I suggested she talk to a sales person in a department store or a dress shop, giving her an idea of the kind of organization she was interviewing with, the kind of position she was seeking, and the amount of money she wanted to spend.* ✱

If you believe your own wardrobe is inadequate, visit a good clothing store and tell them what you're looking for. Make your request comprehensive. Say, for instance, "This is the kind of job I'm interviewing for and I need everything for $200: shoes, stockings, accessories, everything." The sales person should be able to put together two or three outfits for you to select from, but plan on at least two trips to complete the job.

Another tip, if you are an older person. "Look as young as possible," according to Gary Kravetz, owner of National Career Choices, an executive and technical employee recruiting company. If you have gray hair and a few wrinkles, at least look young at heart, and act that way, he advises. Don't overdo it, but don't come across as old and tired. "Enthusiasm helps," he says, and a brand new computer science degree is worth touting.

Mastering the art of interviewing is essential to your successful job search. If you can relax and enjoy it, so much the better. But first and foremost, you must practice and become good at it!

✳ *All her preparation did not prevent Madeline's palms from sweating, but it did give her the presence of mind during the interview to evaluate whether this organization met her employment needs rather than worrying about what she was going to be asked next. By the end of the hour, to her surprise, she was enjoying herself. As she left, she was told a final decision would be made within the week and she would be contacted. She left with confidence. It was justified. A week later the interviewer called Madeline and offered her the position. But that is not the end of her story.*

As we reviewed the job offer, Madeline paused.

"Ever since the interview, I've been thinking about the new food service division. If it's going to be successful, the employees are going to need a lot of training, and right away. I wonder if they've thought about that?"

"Maybe not. Why not bring it up in your letter of acceptance?"

She did and was asked to come in for another interview, this time specifically to discuss her ideas about a training program. The company was impressed. She was asked to help develop the new program and was appointed its first director. Madeline is now proud of herself, proud of her job, a valued employee, and a great pride to her family.

Madeline is a classic example of a career seeker who starts a search aiming toward one goal and midstream adjusts that original goal to accommodate the new insights generated while working through The Professional Self Model. ✳

Fifty Questions Frequently Asked at Interviews

1. What can I do for you?
2. Why did you contact me?
3. Why do you want to work for us?
4. What can you do for us?
5. How do you think you would fit into our operations?
6. What do you know about our company?
7. Tell me about yourself.
8. Have you any experience in supervision?
9. How did you get into your field?
10. Does your employer know that you are planning to leave?
11. Why do you want to leave your present position? Why did you leave your last job?
12. Have you ever been fired from a job? Why? or Why not?
13. Why have you been unemployed for so long?
14. Why have you held so many jobs?
15. What was your salary in your previous position?
16. What are your current salary requirements?
17. Why do you want to change fields now?
18. Don't you feel you're a little too old for this job? (Or a little too young?
19. Aren't you overqualified for this position?
20. What are your general feelings about _____*?
    *(Women in business, unions, sales, production, personnel, management, politics?)
21. Do you have any objections to a psychological interview and tests?
22. What is your philosophy of life?
23. Have you ever thought about going into business for yourself? Would you like to go into business for yourself again if the opportunity were right?

24. What goals did you set for yourself this year and how well have you done toward accomplishing them? Why?
25. What are your professional 5-year goals?
26. What are your personal 5-year goals?
27. How was the (last employer) company as a place to work?
28. What did you like best about your old job? What did you like least?
29. What would you rather have done more of in your last position? Why?
30. If you could have made one suggestion to management in your last job, what would it have been? Why?
31. What do you consider your worst/best attribute?
32. What was the hardest thing you've ever done? Why?
33. What do you regard as your strongest qualification for this job?
34. What do you think is likely to make the difference between success and failure in this position?
35. What do you feel has been your greatest accomplishment in life? Why?
36. What have been your three most noteworthy accomplishments in the past year? Why?
37. What has been your greatest disappointment? Why?
38. What are three of your strongest points? What are three of your weakest points?
39. What have you done in the past year to improve yourself?
40. What factors in your past have contributed most to your development?
41. What factors would you say may have been handicaps in preventing your from moving ahead more quickly?
42. What is your family status?
43. How does your spouse feel about your application for this job?

44. How does your family like your being away from home on extensive business trips?
45. Would you mind moving away from this area?
46. How would you solve this problem of ours?
47. What qualities do you think this company should look for in an applicant for this position?
48. As an employee, what can management do to assist you in functioning effectively?
49. If you are hired, how do you visualize your future with this company?
50. Do you have any other questions?

Sixteen Attributes Sought by Employers

The National Association of Colleges and Employers has listed sixteen attributes employers are looking for. No one interviewer will cover all of these attributes, but they are good indicators of what the selection process is all about and how you can plan for the interview.

Ability to Communicate. Do you have the ability to organize your thoughts effectively? Can you express them clearly when speaking or writing? Are you persuasive?

Intelligence. Do you have the ability to understand and conduct the job assignment? Can you learn the specific operations? Will you be able to contribute original ideas or actions?

Self-Confidence. Are you mature? Can you deal positively and effectively with situations and people? Are you secure about your abilities?

Willingness to Accept Responsibility. Can you recognize what needs to be done and set about doing it?

Initiative. Do you have the ability to identify the purpose for work and to take action? Can you set goals and objectives?

Leadership. Can you guide and direct others to obtain the recognized objectives.?

Energy Level. Do you demonstrate a forcefulness and capacity to move things ahead? Can you maintain your work effort over a period of time and at a sustained rate?

Imagination. Can you conceptualize new situations and form solutions to them? Do you find new answers in standard approaches to problems?

Flexibility. Are you capable of changing? Are you receptive to new ways of doing things, new locations, new people?

Interpersonal Skills. Can you bring out the best in people so they become effective, enthusiastic members of the work team?

Self-Knowledge. Can you realistically assess your capabilities? Can you identify your strengths and weaknesses? Do you know what skills you bring to a job?

Ability to Handle Conflict. Can you contend with stress situations and antagonism? Can you resolve conflicts with others without personal attacks? Do you have a practiced approach to conflict-resolution?

Competitiveness. Do you have a willingness to be measured by your performance in relation to that of others?

Goal Achievement. Can you identify goals and work toward them? Are you challenged by goals?

Skills. Do you have the right combination of education (or training) and skills required for the job you are seeking? Are your skills up to date?

Direction. Have you determined your personal values and needs? Have you reflected on your interests? Have you determined what type of job or occupation will satisfy these things, plus your skills and goals?

"There's an old story about three workers breaking up rocks. When the first was asked what he was doing, he replied, 'Making little ones out of big ones;' the second said, 'Making a living;' and the third, 'Building a cathedral.'" – John Julian Ryan

"If people feel they have control over their destinies they will persist at tasks." – Tom Peters and Robert Waterman

"Job-hunting is stressful, time-consuming, labor-intensive, and low-paying." – Scott Badler

"I think I'll work all my life. When you're having fun, why stop having fun?" – Helen Thomas

10 Negotiating
The slow dance of job search

*"Knowing what to go for, when
to go for it, when to back off."*

An initial offer of the minimum package is not unusual.
Whether or not you can move beyond this depends on
your skills and experience, and the employer's flexibility. Asking for what you want is probably the most difficult step
in the job search process, whether you're a secretary or a division
manager. Whatever your level, the steps and principles are the
same.

- Determine what's feasible
- Identify what you want
- Discuss your requirements
- Plan your strategy
- Present your plan
- Identify your allies
- Reintroduce the remaining topics
- Evaluate the offer
- Follow up
- Reinforce the negotiated topics

✳ *A prestigious San Francisco medical group had offered Dr. Robert Moffett a position as a staff surgeon, and he knew he wanted the
job. He had grown up in the Bay Area and wanted to return. The facility*

was close to the University of California at San Francisco Medical School and the University of California at Berkeley, both first class research institutions, and he wanted to stay on the cutting edge of his field.

"One of the reasons I chose surgery," he confided, "is because nine times out of ten the patients are unconscious when I deal with them. I'm not good at talking. And especially, I'm not good at asking for things like money," admitted this tall, lanky, 36-year-old African American, who had the quiet, disciplined look of a trusted doctor.

"Here's the thing." He leaned forward, bracing his elbows on his knees and pressing his palms together. "I know I'm good at what I do and I know they want me, but all they offered was the minimum package." He ticked off the items on his fingers. "Entry-level salary, four weeks vacation, one week continuing medical education, and medical, dental, and retirement plans." ✳

Negotiation involves a proposal, or series of proposals, regarding what you want, coupled with how that will benefit the new organization.

Negotiating is not:
A monologue.
A battle of wits.
A debate.
A popularity contest.

And above all, negotiating is not a spontaneous event. It takes careful planning and that begins before your initial interview. You will want to go after the highest possible salary both you and the job are worth. The actual figure is irrelevant. What matters is how you will stack up against your peers in terms of prestige and importance to the company. Make a point to find out what benefits the company has, and try to get yourself included in the highest-level ones you can possibly qualify for.

Send Up a Trial Balloon
Discuss Your Requirements

As you plan your own negotiating strategy, research the market value of your own skills by calling your trade association or look in your trade publications. Contact employment agencies and executive recruiters. Ask others in the field about going rates. Make a trip to the library for books and magazine articles with detailed surveys listing current salaries by job description, experience level and location. Check the Help Wanted ads. This will give you an idea of where the job you are looking at stands in relation to the rest in the field.

Strengthen your bargaining position by learning all you can about the job in relation to the company. During your initial interview keep on the lookout for what's been happening in this position. Is the interim department head doing an acceptable job or is the company getting desperate for a replacement? How long has the position been open? How often does it turn over? Have prior offers been made and turned down? What are the specific concerns of the organization and the interviewer? Your first interview should focus on gathering information about the company and selling yourself. Don't set up roadblocks. Once the company has decided to hire you, you can discuss the details.

Next you must know what you want from the job offer. Don't think pie-in-the-sky, but rather ask yourself: "Based on what I know of the market and this company, what should I reasonably expect from this organization?" Be as objective as you can. Then ask yourself, "Why am I worth this?" It's not uncommon to have unrealistic expectations and exaggerated notions of your worth to potential employers and a reality check about now is a good idea. To successfully negotiate, you must create a win-win situation and communicate the benefits of your proposal to the employer.

Once you've identified all the specific items you feel are appropriate, put them down in writing. This gives you a scorecard to use throughout the negotiating process that tells you what you've accomplished, and what is still on the table.

At your final interview, raise the issues you've identified as important to you and relate these to what the boss sees as valuable. Get a feel for what might and might not be acceptable.

✳ *Dr. Bob had put a lot of thought into each of the items he wanted. He listed five:*

> *1. Ten percent additional salary.*
> *2. Two additional weeks vacation.*
> *3. One additional week continuing medical*
> *   education.*
> *4. Two years paid malpractice insurance.*
> *5. Training in microscopic surgery.*

"I've been thinking about this move for over a year," Dr. Bob replied. "I've had a eye open for opportunities listed in my medical journals, and before I came out here for the interview I did some checking around locally. As far as salary goes, the offer is about right for an entry level person with no experience, but I spent four years as a resident at Cook County Hospital in Chicago. I think that puts me at least one step beyond entry level," he insisted. He knew the stress level he had experienced in Chicago and felt the extra vacation time was necessary to alleviate that. The malpractice insurance and continuing education were not unusual perks.

But it was the microscopic surgery was especially important to him.

"I didn't even bring it up at the interview. I was just into reacting to their questions, and I was too nervous to even mention it." He paused. "One of the reasons this invitation excites me is that one of the associates is perfecting a microscopic surgery technique that is way beyond what anyone else is doing here. If I could just train under him...," his fingers itched in anticipation. ✳

Salaries are often the least negotiable, but benefits, personal time, parking, education, bonuses, and moving costs are all fair game. (You'll find a more complete list of commonly negotiated items at the end of this chapter.)

Remember, most employers offer new hires the minimal financial and benefits package they can get by with. And why not? It makes good business sense for the employer. You need to ask yourself if it makes good business sense for you. From your research identify what is acceptable and what you want changed. Note what is acceptable, what is out of the question, and what is still possible and/or important to you.

Put Your Terms on the Table
Presenting Your Plan

The employer will try to make the job offer a one-time event. But once the offer has been made, you need to evaluate it against your requirements. Don't be afraid to ask for what you feel you're worth, as long as it's within generally accepted limits for your age and experience. Many employers are reluctant to negotiate salaries upwards prior to seeing you perform, but remember your strongest bargaining position is before you say "yes," and that subsequent raises and bonuses are likely to be based on this first figure.

✶ *Saying what he wanted and actually moving forward with his proposals were two entirely different things. Just thinking about a confrontation made him break out in a nervous sweat. Yet he knew from experience that accepting the first offer without question would leave him with the uncomfortable feeling he had been taken advantage of. Now he felt his requests were reasonable and his goal of training with the surgeon was too important to his future to let it slip away by default.*

In his written response to the offer, Dr. Bob began by stressing his interest in the position. He next indicated there were several matters he would like to discuss with the senior partners. ✶

Thank You, But May We Talk Some More?
Introduce the Remaining Topics

Respond to any offer in writing. Establish as quickly as possible your desire to accept the position. This is key to any successful negotiation. Also establish quickly the parts of the offer you will accept and agree to. Then carefully state your desires. Do not discuss why you want them. At this initial stage you just need to let them know what you want. When you meet with the principals, all of these will be negotiable and open for discussion. The outcome will depend on the acceptability of your reasoning and the flexibility of the employer. Your reasons for the requests will generate dialogue and discussion during your next meeting.

Identify Your Allies
Who Will Make the Decision?

Now identify who in the organization can make the changes you want to come about. It probably isn't the personnel department. Is it the person who interviewed you? Is it the direct supervisor, if that is someone different? Is it someone higher up? If you are working with a recruiter or employment agency, use them to feel out the company as to how much negotiating room there is. It's possible the employer has some hard constraints in some areas and flexibility in others. As you respond in writing to this initial offer, be sure your requests are within the realm of possibility for the company. Ask that the decision makers be present at the next interview.

    ✱ *"Who actually made you the offer?" I asked.*
    "The Personnel Director," he replied.
    "The Personnel Director won't have the authority to change anything. Why don't you set your agenda down in a memo and recommend the full partners review it?" ✱

Preparation, practice and presentation are the keys to successful negotiating. You will need to be prepared to present your requirements with enough information about yourself and your qualifications to justify your request. The employer assumes you are a hard worker and that you learn quickly, so these arguments won't get you much. It is paramount that you prepare your materials, arguments and strategies in a manner that stresses the potential benefits to the organization. You must convince the interviewer that your unique experience and/or expertise will benefit the company more than any other candidate. Strengthen your position by quantifying those benefits in terms of dollars, either earned or saved. Put your reasoning down on paper. This clarifies your thinking.

✳ *I now asked Dr. Bob to outline for himself a script consisting of point-by-point justification for his requests. This gave him the psychological lift he needed to overcome the lack of confidence in his communication skills and created a "comfort zone" for conversation during his meetings with the partners.* ✳

Now is the time to practice your presentation much as you did for the initial interview. Making yourself comfortable with your presentation is even more important now.

When you meet with the decision makers, reiterate your desire to accept the position, and those parts of the offer you both agree on. Remind them of your qualifications. Remember that demonstrated experience and tested skills count for a whole lot more than potential or promise. Through your presentation you will want to alert and excite the employer with your potential, but your agenda should keep focused on the solid evidence of your current worth.

This additional information gives you control over the agenda during the meeting. It helps the organization decide the merits of your requirements and gives you a certain amount of leverage. When you are in the driver's seat, it's easier to communicate your confidence in yourself. This in turn affects how others perceive you.

✻ The three senior partners agreed to meet with Dr. Bob. His initial excitement dissipated when they totally stonewalled him on the salary issue.

"We think this is a fair starting salary for a new person entering our practice," Dr. Noland, the spokesman, told the young physician following his presentation. "And six weeks vacation is just too much," he shook his head. "However, we are prepared to extend your continuing medical education benefit an additional two weeks."

They also offered to pay his malpractice insurance the first year.

"But we don't see the value of training a second microsurgery specialist at this time," Dr. Noland concluded. ✻

What Have You Gained? What Have You Lost?
Evaluating the Counter Offer

Once a counter offer has been made, regroup. First look at the points the company agreed to. Again list the points still to be resolved. Evaluate the offer carefully. Sometimes your needs will be met, but not in the form originally requested. You need to assess exactly what an alternative does for you.

✻ Back in my office, I pointed out to a discouraged Dr. Bob that all was not lost and this was not necessarily their final offer, nor was it his.

Dr. Bob accepted this intellectually, but internally, his stress level soared. He waffled between his adamant position to continue the process, to fearing he had nuked the entire deal. He needed patience, stress management, and a certain amount of plain old courage to get him through. Throughout college, Dr. Bob had been a long-distance runner. I encouraged him to take this up again to decrease the stress, but the courage would have to come from Dr. Bob's own conviction of his agenda.

When Dr. Bob took a second look at the offer from a calmer perspective, he could see progress.

"Picking up the malpractice insurance will save me $20,000 the first year," he admitted. "I guess I can accept the salary. I can put the

difference towards my student loans, which I was worried about to begin with."

"I know you're disappointed they won't look at more vacation time, but," I pointed out, "two extra weeks for continuing medical education effectively adds two more weeks away from the stress of the office."

He nodded in agreement. ✶

Learn to view the negotiating process in a detached, analytical, unemotional way. Regard the rejection of any of your original demands impersonally, not as a individual slight. Continue to concentrate on how what you want benefits the organization, and how you will make a difference. Focus your justifications on your interests in the work, not on the position, salary or benefits to you. Generate lots of possibilities for accomplishing your desires before issuing the "bottom line ultimatum." When you develop possible solutions, you present yourself as a creative problem solver with vision. You become an active participant in your own career future.

✶ *For the next week we focused on Dr. Bob's counter offer: what he was going to present to the partners and how was he going to present it in a way that demonstrated value to the group. Again I asked him to do this in writing. Here is his working list. From this he developed his comments for the next meeting.*

1. *This specialization is new and unique to this area. In all probability new clients will be generated above and beyond what can be handled by Dr. Abbott, the current specialist, alone.*
2. *It is also a high profit procedure and a second specialist will be able to produce significant additional revenue.*
3. *A generation exists between Dr. Abbott and myself. By the time I finish my training and develop a reputation in the specialty, he will be approaching retirement. When he does, you'll have to replace him. If I'm already be on board and trained, there'll be no need for an expensive and time consuming recruitment effort.*
4. *I have the potential for success. My academic and surgical expertise demonstrated this during my residency.* ✶

Head 'Em Off at the Pass and Call in the Big Guns
Identify the Road Blocks

At this stage you must identify any stumbling blocks. Use your resources and contact all potential allies to address and overcome these. Ask your references to contact decision makers. If you have contacts within the organization, explore how they can help you. Your job now is to provide as many answers as you can to the questions you know will come up, covering as many "what ifs" and "yes, buts" as you can think of.

* When Dr. Bob and I met again, we were coming down to the wire. We looked at what he needed to do to increase his acceptability to the partners. Now was the time to enlist his allies in the medical group. Dr. Bob had spoken to Dr. Abbott, the specialist, as soon as the firm had expressed an interest in him. Dr. Abbott had agreed to take him on as an intern providing Dr. Bob could convince the partners to accept the arrangement. Now Dr. Bob solicited his active support, asking him to speak to the partners on his behalf.

Dr. Bob met with the surgical specialist, and gave him a list of the points he had previously made. He asked him to speak to the partners as soon as possible so that when they met the following week with Dr. Bob they would have had as much time as possible to consider the specialist's input before coming to their decision. *

The bottom line for the employer is still getting the best person for the least amount of dollars or the least amount of hassle. Keep the discussion focused on the benefits to the company.

* Dr. Bob needed to convince the partners he was worth the extras he was asking for, that it was in their best interest to consider his request. All the while he continued to stress his interest in joining this particular practice. Dr. Bob accurately perceived the hostility of one of the partners. He needed to turn him around.

We took a determined look at what this doctor might be reacting to. Dr. Bob felt that to the doctor he appeared to be a pretentious young upstart right out of medical school who had an inflated opinion of his worth. To change his mind, Dr. Bob needed to convince him of the positive benefits his experience would bring to the firm.

"Why not take the bull by the horns," I suggested. "Ask for a meeting and get to know him on a one-to-one basis."

Because of the hostility, Dr. Bob hesitated. He was sure the doctor would have nothing to do with him. And even if he did, he wasn't sure he was up to the confrontation. On the other hand, I pointed out, nothing ventured, nothing gained. To his surprise the doctor accepted his invitation for lunch. They met the following day and Dr. Hollister spoke quite candidly.

"You impress me as an arrogant opportunist. Don't you think you're being presumptuous?" he asked flat out.

"Not really, sir," Dr. Bob began, his stomach rebelling against the antagonism. It was too late to leave, so he might as well tough it out and give it his best shot, he thought.

"The pace, the variety, the volume of cases I handled in Chicago places me in more than an entry level category. I proved my worth there, and I bring this experience to your practice. I appreciate all you have agreed to so far. I have some heavy educational debts. They run in the neighborhood of $100,000 and they trouble me. My family was very supportive when I went to medical school, but not in a financial way. My student loans are coming due in the next four years, and I won't default on them." He paused a moment, then looked up, grinned and added, "My father would kill me." He then turned to the key subject.

"It's the opportunity of working with Dr. Abbott that makes joining this practice so important to me. His technique has fascinated me since I first read about it in the JAMA Journal at school. This technology will help solve a number of medical problems in their early stages. That's what really excites me."

The doctor came away with a better understanding of Dr. Bob's position and confirmed that he was the hold out. While making no commitment, he assured Dr. Bob he would take this new information into consideration.

"By and large I feel this is a good match," Dr. Bob began the next meeting with the partners. "I am deeply convinced the expertise I developed during my Cook County Hospital residency will strengthen this practice."

After he had stressed the matters he felt they agreed on, he pressed on to the one unresolved item, the one of primary importance to him: a one-year training program with Dr. Abbott.

"I know I will personally gain a great deal from this," he acknowledged.

"Now let's consider it from your side of the table. I believe you are risking very little in allowing me to do this," and he outlined why he felt this would benefit the entire practice, using the working list he developed earlier. *"I believe what I am asking has only positive outcomes for everyone,"* he reiterated.

The meeting ended with the partners appearing fairly comfortable that they were reaching common ground but feeling they needed to discuss his interest in training for this specialization with other members of the staff, before making a final offer the following week.

When the panel met with Dr. Bob the meeting was short and to the point.

"This is what we are offering you. Please review it and give us your decision on Friday," Dr. Noland told him. ✱

When the final offer is made, you may either accept or reject. Look it over carefully to assure yourself you are making the right decision.

✱ *"Man-o-man, will you look at this?"* I could see he was pleased with himself as he handed me the proposal.

The offer included the original salary and vacation, the additional two weeks of continuing education, and the first year's premium on his malpractice insurance. The partners had finally agreed to the training program, based on Dr. Abbott's recommendation and support, but only after Dr. Bob had worked six months as a general surgeon, the position originally offered. For the next eighteen months he would spend fifty percent of his time with the specialist as his assistant, learning the new surgical technique. Following that, if he passed the qualifying exam, he was to commit to remaining with the partnership for a minimum of two more years when he would be considered for an associate partnership.

"This is really excellent. You've done a great job," I congratulated him.

"All I need to do now is sign and return it."

"Not so fast!" I cautioned. ✱

Put It In Writing
Follow Up

If you accept the offer, make sure you understand exactly what you are going to commit to. It's in your best interest to be responsible for coming up with the final draft of what you believe has been decided. Then, if there is some misunderstanding, the employer must come to you for clarification as opposed to you going to them. The ball is now in their court, where it should be.

✳ *"In some of our first discussions you told me that independence was an important value to you. I feel it is crucial for you to recognize that you are essentially committing yourself to that organization for four years: six months of full-time general surgery, plus the eighteen months of training in the specialization and an additional two years after that."*

Dr. Bob needed to see that although he had been offered much of what he wanted, there were strings attached, and he needed to be comfortable with those strings if the partners were going to make this considerable investment of time, energy, training and money.

"Yes, I think this is an offer I can live with," he told me the next day. "It is a four year commitment. It means putting off my own private practice for at least that long. And if I decide on that, I'll have to practice somewhere else. That's part of the package, too. They don't want to train a competitor. On the other hand, in one way or another, I've got everything I asked for, and in the case of the training, even more. I would say this is very fair, very fair indeed. In four years I might find a partnership offer very desirable." ✳

Negotiations eventually boil down to a matter of two or three meetings where you give and take, you win some, you lose some, and at some point you come to a middle ground. At this time you have to agree or disagree. Nine times out of ten, you will get some of what you ask for. Now you either accept the employment and terms you've agreed upon so far, or you don't, thank

them very much for their thoughtful consideration, and move on
with your life.

✻ *Dr. Bob called Dr. Noland, thanked him for the offer, and said he
was accepting it. He told him he would be submitting the offer as he
understood it in writing, so that if there was any misunderstanding it
could be cleared up immediately.*

*We drafted the acceptance letter and sent it over by messenger
that day. The partners reviewed it and agreed as it was presented. The
contract was drawn up accordingly. When it was signed, all parties
walked away feeling that although each had given some, each had made
an excellent deal.* ✻

Common Negotiable Items

A signing bonus
An annual performance bonus
Bonus program based on meeting specific performance goals
A severance settlement
The right to do freelance work on your own time
Cost of moving
Low interest loans
Company-paid pension plan
Paid-up life insurance
Health-club, country club and/or private club membership
Service and professional club memberships
First class air travel
Airline VIP clubs
Spouse's travel expenses
Extra vacation time
Sabbatical leaves
Annual physical examination
Child care/parental leave
Personal time
Education
Stock options
A larger or better office
A reserved place in the company parking lot
Deferred compensation
A company car
Reimbursement for entertaining at home
Expense account
Flexible work schedule
Part-time/job sharing
Retirement plans
Profit sharing
Paid trips

"I think most of us are looking for a calling, not a job." – Studs Terkel

"Work is much more fun than fun." – Noel Coward

"Career and identity are inextricably bound up: Indeed they are almost equivalent." – Douglas LaBier

"The policeman is the little boy who grew up to be what he said he was going to be." – Raymond Burr

11 Establishing Your Time Line
Setting a realistic schedule

> *"Risk is the price of admission*
> *as you begin your search for a*
> *more fulfilling career."*

Whenever you launch a new job search, it is important to establish a realistic time line. To imagine you will find the job of your dreams before the rent comes due is not only unrealistic, it sets you up for failure – definitely a blow, often a crippling one, to your self esteem. Each step takes time, and therefore patience. If each is done thoroughly you will position yourself not only for this career change, but for all future moves.

Begin this process of career exploration gently. "Think of your career as a journey of discovery, not a climb up some organizational ladder," suggest Stephen M. Polan and Mark Levine in *Worth* magazine. "There's no predetermined path. Your career is a series of moves from project to project, employer to employer, even industry to industry. Each project should be exciting to contemplate."

Talk with people, volunteer your time, take on an internship in an industry that interests you. Ask to tag along with someone for a day at their job and observe the actual operations of the occupation. It's paramount that this step in the process be approached cautiously and with time for reflection. It may take a number of forays into different industries or employment situations before you can comfortably decide on one.

When I first moved to Santa Barbara, I interned with an art gallery. I had a fantasy of owning and operating my own gallery. Three weeks into the internship, it was clear I was not interested nor did I have the personality for the management functions of ownership, much less the skills to handle the financial aspects. I was attracted to the glamour of owning an art gallery, not the reality of the business. When my internship ended, I happily regressed to being an admirer of art and remain so to this day. That was a reality check, and it is a very important aspect of decision making for people making mid-life career changes.

As with other areas in our lives there are no guarantees in this process. You simply put forth your best effort, weigh your options, and then decide.

Figler suggests that eighty percent of your work will consist of "detective work" or "behind the scenes" work to establish a foundation for a successful career change and job search. As we have said oft before, research is the key. Much of this involves reading books, magazines, newspapers and employee literature to establish a frame of reference for determining where to place your focus.

You will also spend time on self discovery. When I work with individual clients through the Personal Assessment phase, I require them to keep a career journal and regularly record their thoughts regarding the process and what they are learning about themselves. All of this culminates in the realization of a new persona, your Professional Self.

It is important that you do take the time to incorporate all aspects of this process. Your long-term goal is not just to find another job, but to establish your Professional Self through this self-discovery process. This often involves changes in your basic attitude about yourself as a working person. A positive attitude lets you ask "What opportunities does this current situation present that the old one didn't?" In this economy there are far more opportunities to become your own boss, to turn your interests and hobbies into money-making ventures, and to develop areas of knowledge that give you additional opportunities in the future.

If you need help gaining perspective or with an attitude adjustment, seek the help of career professionals. They can help you process your options, as well as your fears, anger, and all the other emotions that play a critical role in this effort. This job market is not for sissies or the unprepared. Do your homework. Ask for help. Consider your options. Then proceed.

As you progress, you will also develop a new, updated vocabulary for describing yourself in the work world. This vocabulary will sound more fluent, descriptive and authentic as you move along.

You probably won't notice these changes at first, but as a career counselor I can assure you that I quickly begin to hear these changes in my clients' descriptions of themselves. I see ongoing evidence of their taking control, of feeling more powerful, of becoming more sophisticated job searchers. After perhaps weeks of what looks to you like unproductive effort, suddenly you become aware that you are making more knowledgeable decisions about the direction your career is taking. You see how best to use your time in each aspect of the process and to look forward to a time when the process will come to a successful conclusion.

To help you gauge yourself, take a look at the suggested time lines at the end of the chapter. The first sets the pace if you are exploring a new career, the second if change has found you and your first priority is immediate employment.

Don't Jump Ship
Employed People Make Stronger Candidates

If you are employed, I encourage you to stay that way until you've accepted another offer. It's difficult to look for work when you are holding down another job, but it's infinitely harder if you're without a paycheck. Unemployment not only brings about its own stress, it encourages you to rush the process. If you are unhappy where you are, try to restructure the job as best you can to minimize the bad and maximize the good. Look closely at personality styles (Chapter 5) for some suggestions.

The other advantage to being employed goes to an old adage: "'Em 'at has, gits." Interviewers tend to look upon the employed as seeking new opportunities and the unemployed as desperate for work.

Help is Out There
From the Feds to Your Next Door Neighbor

And then there's the money part. If you've been laid off, your first agenda item is a trip to the nearest state employment office. Not only will you register for unemployment insurance, but you'll file a job application that will be entered into your state's system. California's Job Match system, for instance, is a statewide computer network matching vacancies with suitable applicants locally, regionally and statewide. The Kansas Job Service offers two-day job search workshops, as well as one-on-one vocational counseling and aptitude testing. Your next step is to visit any federal training or jobs programs in your area, such as the Job Training Network. Both state and federal programs often offer job search workshops that can be very helpful as well.

For the worker displaced by "downsizing," the feds fund programs under the Economically Displaced Workers Assistance Act. In California, under this program, some thirty Experience Unlimited job clubs have been established by the California Employment Development Department. Restricted to those with two years of college or equivalent education, and those looking for technical, management or other professional employment, the clubs act essentially as a member-operated employment agency.

Uncle Sam isn't your only source of help. The American Association of Retired Persons offers AARP WORKS, a series of eight workshops on employment planning for older adults. Forty Plus is another self-help organization for professional and managerial employees age forty and older.

If you have a computer and an on-line service, check out the career and job search forums. You can list your resume, review employers looking for new people, ask questions on a forum, and get free information on resume writing and interviewing techniques. You'll also find a number of publications and services available for a fee. Once you have determined the Internet is a fruitful venue for your search, there are a number of books, as well as how-to seminars available.

Now's the time to network big-time. Jack Erdlen, chief executive officer of The Erdlen Bograd Group, an outplacement and human resources consulting firm headquartered in Wellesley, Massachusetts, suggests you begin by making a list of everyone you know. Like everyone – from the CEO's you've worked with, to your clergyman, to the person you buy your burgers from. Then sort them in the most likely order of "hearing about jobs" and start making those contacts.

Next you must look to your budget. List your mortgage or rent payment, utilities, insurance, car loan, food, gasoline, job-hunting costs. Pay only these, advocates twice-fired Jane Bryant Quinn. Put your other bills in a box marked "later," she says. Next add up your income. If there is a gap, see how long your cash reserves will last. Consider a home-equity loan to give yourself some extra cash. "Your goal is to cover basic expenses for at least nine months while you hunt for work," she advises.

Watch out for rip-offs. Resume writing, job-hunting services and the like can come at a high price with little results. Check out exactly what you are buying before you plunk down those precious dollars. If you decide to hire a consultant, the best way to do so is armed with references from colleagues or friends. Even then, make sure you ask lots of questions. Meanwhile, check out your nearest adult education center and your alumni career center.

"Always ask: 'What concrete, in-hand material will I be provided with and what knowledge will I walk away with?'" advises Benita Ugoline, owner of Career Architect, a job search training company.

It is important you give yourself the time and mental energy it takes to identify, search out, and land a new job. Although a great deal of your efforts now will be active rather than introspective, it is a good time to take stock, by necessity perhaps rather than choice, of the things that will be important for you to consider as you look for a new job.

To cover the cash flow gap, and abate your stress, look for part-time work. It's often easier to get and it allows you time to pursue more substantial full-time work. Today even professionals are getting into the act. Interim, a Fort Lauderdale, Florida-based temporary agency offers temporary doctors, lawyers, paralegals, accountants and other skilled professionals, at wages as high as $42.50 an hour. By taking a temporary assignment, you will still be a member of the work force, but your part-time status will be a constant reminder that this is only temporary. Your long range goal is full time employment.

The Awful Truth
There Ain't No Free Lunch

Changing careers requires thought and courage, and should not be entered into lightly. One of the realities of moving from a field where you have proved yourself to something entirely different, is that you are not likely to receive your old salary. Sometimes you need to sacrifice in the short term in order to realize your maximum long-range potential. Can you live with what you are offered?

✳ *Ellie Fairchild came back to see me when she received the job offer from a Nevada radio station.*

"Congratulations. It looks like you've done just exactly what you set out to do."

"Yes, that's true," she admitted. "But there is a downside."

"Oh?"

"My salary will be about half of what I make at the department store."

"A hard choice, but not at all unusual," I assured her.

Ellie spent some time thoroughly reviewing and evaluating her options. She decided to accept the job, but not without some stomach fluttering and finger crossing.

Her gamble paid off. Within three years she had achieved her old salary level. She felt professionally satisfied and fulfilled. ✳

Allow yourself time to seek advice, venture into new areas, mull over your options and eliminate those that no longer meet your requirements. Seek out job fairs. Offer potential employers a copy of your resume. Give them a bit of background on yourself, and ask lots of questions. Find out all you can. Send thank-you notes to everyone who gives you the time of day.

Trial and error is a good teacher. Chances are the first career change you decide upon will not turn out. It is usually the third or fourth option you explore that turns out to be the best. Don't despair, your work on the ones you discard is part of the process and is in no way a waste of time!

✳ *Kevin Avalos had worked in the computer information system of the banking industry for ten years. He felt unfulfilled and couldn't see himself in banking for the rest of his work life.*

The first interest area he explored involved working in the training and development department of an organization providing in-house seminars to employees. He liked the idea of more contact with people, of being an expert and of providing a service. After extensive library research, conducting informational interviews and actually going to three job interviews, he realized that although he liked the majority of the work, he did not look forward to the notion of being "on stage" everyday, as he would be in a seminar atmosphere.

His second search took him into the area of consulting with emphasis on his computer expertise, but again this was too much like what he was doing at the bank. While exploring this area, he interned with a consultant who had been hired by an accounting firm to upgrade its computer system. Kevin found himself attracted to the accounting field and began the process of retraining to support a change in that direction. By this time he had accepted a transfer by the bank to a smaller community. As he continued his accounting preparation he developed an internship with a major accounting firm in his new community during tax season. Because of the size of the community, the accounting firm was smaller than he would have considered in his old neighborhood. This gave him the opportunity to work closely with the principals of the firm, and conversely, for them to observe him at close range. They were impressed with what they saw, and offered him a full time position. They even agreed to give him time off to prepare for the Certified Public Accountant exam.

It took Kevin two full years to move from computers to accounting. During that time he continued his job at the bank and explored his options in the evenings and on weekends. Exploring the two aborted areas gave him confidence that accounting was the best career choice for him at this point in his life. He was able to pinpoint just exactly what he wanted from his new career: the opportunity to demonstrate expertise in a highly technical and specialized area, and to work independently while allowing contact with clients and co-workers as the need arose. ✱

At This Point in Time
Determining Where You Are and What You Need to Do

You may not need to go through the entire Professional Self Model because you come to it having done some work already. The joy of this model is that you can enter from any place you happen to be along the career development continuum.

Some aspects will take longer than others, depending on where you are. Reentry people, for example, usually need a great deal of emphasis on the Personal Assessment section. People that have significant work experience in one career area and are now changing directions usually need very little time on this because they are fairly clear on their values, interests, and skills. Their emphasis will be on the research portion of the model.

If returning to a formal program is not reasonable, either for financial or time constraints, explore evening extension programs at your nearest university or college. Many offer certificate programs at a fraction of the time and cost of an additional degree. Some professional associations also offer training and certificate programs. Look for computer training through adult education programs or your local computer store.

For every job seeker and career changer now is a good time to review your skills and identify those that need updating. Middle managers may need to learn new leadership styles. Engineers must become more "human," humanists must become more technically literate. Everyone must be competent with the tools of the computing and advanced telecommunications age.

Your marketing tools will need reworking, since with each new job search you will want your resume and all other marketing tools to confirm the new position.

Check Point Charlie
Keeping Yourself on Track

As you begin this career change process it is essential to set some obvious check points along the way. Once a month you should evaluate what you've accomplished. Try writing a statement at the beginning of each month on the current status of your career search, and then what it is you want to achieve during the next month. Put that statement in an envelope and seal it. At the end of the month write another statement about what you have learned and what your attitude is about the process. Compare the two documents and decide your level of progress. How committed are you to career change? Did you work as hard as you intended? Are you frustrated because the answers are not coming as easily as you thought they would? Are you clearer about your Professional Self? These statements not only serve as performance indicators, they also help you pinpoint problem areas.

You may be asking yourself to do too much too soon. You may be overwhelmed with the process. But don't think about giving up. As I stress throughout this book, the kind of change you want to occur does not happen without planning and participation on your part. Finding meaningful work does not "happen" to you, it is a matter of making it "happen" for yourself. So set reasonable, measurable, time-limited goals and evaluate them on a regular basis. Look for ways to make it fun.

Keep in mind as we talk about change, that change is often resisted, typically because people do not feel they have the skills to deal with the new situation. Be patient. Keep going. You are gaining those skills.

Another aspect of any change is the element of risk. Risk of failure. Risk you will be disappointed in yourself. Risk of unforeseen factors and events. Don't let this stop you. Risk is the price of admission as you begin your search for a more fulfilling career. This is the only way you will find out what you have to offer and how much value your work has for others. If you look upon this change as opportunity, as you go on you can expect to feel curiosity, challenge and hopefulness. Stress, helplessness and fragmentation will give way to new creativity, control and commitment.

If you start your career search by identifying your skills, and incorporate all of the components of the Professional Self Model outlined here, your realistic time line for landing a position that meets your needs ranges from eighteen to twenty-four months. If you are unemployed with job search as your number one priority, a commonly accepted rule of thumb is that it will take one month for every $10,000 of salary you expect. The general economy and the industry base of the community you are in will also affect the time it takes for you to be successful. This time line can be shortened if you are working with a career counselor or with a career development group, such as a job club, that will help you monitor your progress and offer advice on short cuts with the process.

To ensure the success of your career search it must be incorporated into your everyday life. If you are working on this while holding down a full-time job, plan on spending no more than two hours a day on your career change. If you are already pounding the pavement, dedicating four hours a day is a better goal, but certainly no more than six. The main thing is to commit to spending a specific amount of time every day at this. Actively engaging yourself in this process will enhance your chances of success and will minimize the time it takes to move from the first steps of the search to accepting a new position.

Work smarter, not harder. Assess how much of this process you are comfortable doing yourself and how much can be done more comfortably or efficiently with the assistance of professionals. Investing in professional career counseling or taking a career search class through your local adult education program may be the best way to overcome personal inertia and ensure an in-depth completion of each task. Being accountable to another is often the push you need to keep you on your schedule. You also get feedback from people who are not closely invested in your career search. This can be very helpful because it is sometimes difficult to get an objective opinion from people who are close to you. Outsiders can often shed a guiding light when you reach a stalemate.

All Work and No Play Makes You Know What
Take Time to Smell the Flowers

Make this search a part of your life, but not all of your life. This is important. Relax, continue your normal routine, but adjust it to incorporate the time needed to conduct a thorough career search. Do not compromise other important aspects of your life, like exercise, during this time. Physical activity is an excellent way to relieve the inevitable stress that builds up. Keep up your social life as well. Friends are especially important at this time.

Reward yourself for small accomplishments and acknowledge the big ones with hats and horns! You are making a big move in your life and this should not be done without some degree of acknowledgment and ceremony.

Try to find a balance between having the patience to let things happen and taking the initiative so things will happen. Every job search calls for a readjustment in this equation, and only through trial and error can you establish this balance.

As you have seen through the friends you have met within these pages, each step takes patience and determination. But each of these colleagues persevered, went head to head with their own fears, addressed the barriers that stood in the way, and accomplished their personal goals. They are living proof the process works; that this investment in yourself pays off. If you haven't already, start today. As you define, refine and establish your Professional Self, you'll know you're worth it!

Estimated Time Line for Career Changers

I. **Months 1 to 4**
   Goals: Assessment/Education/Information
   Activities to consider during this time:
   1. Explore career counseling.
   2. Consider career change courses available through adult education or a college or university in your area.
   3. If you are on your own, work through the exercises on interests, personality styles and values and get to know your Professional Self.
   4. Carefully catalog your skills and choose those you want to carry forward, those you need to acquire.
   5. Identify people who will be supportive of your idea of career change; look to them for comfort, encouragement and advice. Beware of those who may try to sabotage your plans. Remember not everyone likes change for themselves and these people are not willing to encourage it in others.
   6. Establish your personal network.
   7. Develop a reading list of books and magazines that increases your knowledge of careers and job market predictions. Now is the time to meet the reference librarian at your local library who knows where all the good books are located. Frequent the career and business sections of your local book store and create your own career library.
   8. Read your reading list!
   9. Develop a list of possible careers you are willing to consider.
   10. Develop your job search strategies and learn how to look for the work you want.

II. **Months 5 to 10**
   Goals: Investigation/Risk taking/Elimination
   Activities to consider during this time:
   1. Informational interviews.
   2. Active networking within the professional communities you have identified.
   3. Resume development.
   4. Application to viable career positions.
   5. Mock interviews.
   6. Follow-up as necessary with career counselor and/or support people.
   7. Eliminate and reestablish career categories as they surface.

III. **Months 11 to 24**
   Goals: Actual career change
   Activities to consider during this time:
   1. Through process of elimination, identify career area and positions of choice.
   2. Identify concrete steps to move you in that direction.
      a. Retraining.
      b. Internships.
      c. Skill building.
   3. Make connections with people and places that provide experiences to make you employable in your new career.
   4. Apply for positions.
   5. Interview.
   6. Review offers.
   7. Negotiate salary and benefits.
   8. Accept most suitable offer.
   9. Thank your support system.
   10. Celebrate!
   11. Repeat as often as necessary.

Estimated Time Line for Active Job Seekers

I.   **Month 1**
Goals: Motivation/Prioritization/Temporary employment
Activities to consider during this time:

1. Contact the personnel office of your former (or soon to be former) employer.
    a. Inquire as to whether outplacement services are available.
    b. Ask about the procedure for unemployment benefits.
    c. Ask about status of benefits as a result of the lay off.
    d. Visit your local state employment office and your local federal jobs/training programs.

2. Assess your financial needs in order to maintain as familiar a lifestyle as possible. You may need help from a financial planner or a career counselor for a realistic look at this.

3. Based on this information, if immediate employment is your first priority in order to meet monthly expenses, rework your resume.

4. Contact professional search firms and temporary agencies in your area with your resume and let them know you are available. Check out help wanted sections of area newspapers and professional journals.

5. Enlist your support system to help you with mock interviews with immediate part-time employment in mind. (This instantly identifies you as a skilled and talented job seeker which gives you the psychological lift you need at this point, and it helps overcome the immediate feeling of panic.)

6. Contact the local chamber of commerce for economic forecasts and a copy of the business directory in your community to determine what you have to work with in terms of potential employers.

7. Schedule at least four, but no more than six, hours a day actively seeking employment.

8. Refer to Career Change Time Line and incorporate initial activities into your schedule.

II. Months 2 and 3

Goals: Establishing contacts/Job interviews/Maintaining motivation and self-esteem.

Activities to consider during this time:

1. Continued use of your support system in the job search arena.

2. Conduct mailing to family and friends enlisting their help in your search with specific goals and employment agendas.

3. Follow up with phone calls requesting names of potential contacts and employment leads.

4. Continue to polish your resume and interviewing skills as job search becomes more clearly defined.

5. Build into your day a way to have fun and relieve stress.

6. Continue to maintain contacts with professional search firms, responding to their leads with applications and informational interviews.

7. Continue with activities from Career Change Time Line.

III. Months 4 to 6

Goals: Evaluation of employment status/Changing gears/ Full time professional employment

Activities to consider during this time:

1. Continue with activities on Career Change Time Line.

2. Continue to pursue employment opportunities as they arise through your use of search firms, family and friends and leads you obtain through your own research.

3. If full time employment has not been offered by now, take stock of the situation and determine if you need to switch gears. Are you fishing where the fish are? Do you need to find another pond? Do you have the right bait?

4. Work closely with your career support system to fine tune your strategy and validate that you are doing all you can at this time. Make adjustments as necessary until you are successful.

5. Evaluate offers.

6. Negotiate salary and benefits.

7. Accept position.

8. Thank your support system.

9. Celebrate!

10. Repeat as often as necessary.

The Professional Self Model

lifestyle

positioning

planning

perspective

attitude

information

you

job market

job search
strategies

✳

A The Role of the Career Counselor
What to expect

While the majority of my professional experience has been with traditional-age college students, I also work privately with people my age who are emotionally mature, financially grounded, and willing – albeit timidly – to look seriously at career change. They are satisfied with what they have accomplished, but are ready, or forced, to move on. Hardly anyone I know has escaped the downsizing of American enterprise. Many successful middle-aged people are taking stock and re-ordering the rhythm of their lives.

Most of these clients have never before sought the services of a career counselor, and are unsure what to expect. Among their first questions is, "How long will it take?" One of my first challenges is to tell them that the answer to their search lies in a process and is not instantly available in some computer. They must learn to find the answers to their questions by using electronic communication, books and magazines, and by talking to actual people such as reference librarians. John Naisbitt, co-author of the popular *Megatrends* books, writes that the mark of an intelligent person at the end of the twentieth century will not be the amount of information they know, but rather their ability to access information.

I also give my clients materials to complete at home. These are assignments on values, interests, skills and personality styles, much as you have done here. In order to do my job well, I need as much information as I can get from them. While they are collecting information, I am busy observing the process, taking note of the gaps and vulnerable areas of their plans, and assessing the reality of their choices. These career inventories and values exercises provide a point of departure from which we can begin the second phase of our time together.

Rethinking Your World
Act II

During this time, I see their spirits soar as they begin to see new career possibilities. My goal is to create a common knowledge base in order to make our communication more effective and to help put a different slant on their world view. We get used to seeing the world through our own eyes and filtering information through our own unique circumstances. Before decisions are made about future career goals, it is important to take time to reeducate yourself about the world.

＊ *Bill Barnes stormed into my office, his demeanor daring me to disagree.*

"There are no teaching jobs out their for someone with an English degree," he bellowed. "I've sent out a hundred applications, and there are no jobs!"

"Okay," I said. "Why don't you look for something else?"

He stopped in his tracks, and while he was getting his breath, I continued.

"You've done everything you could, and you've discovered there are no teaching jobs in English. Let's look at what other areas your education will take you." ＊

Career changers begin to see a number of options as we move into this new phase, which I refer to as the "career-of-the-week period," where they become aware of some not-so-obvious careers. Each session, they come in with a new plan based on their previous week's reading assignment or interview. This information has expanded their horizon and created a knowledge base from which their ideas and decisions can springboard. Now I can ask questions based on my observations.

As we establish common ground, the hard work starts. We begin to look at their need for change and at their support system. Why do they want to change careers? Can they articulate what they will miss about their current career? What five things are they proud of about their work? Who among their family or friends will be supportive? Who will sabotage their attempts to change? How will people react to them differently based on their new professional identity? How will it feel to not have the power an executive position involves? Will it be worth the less stressful work environment their new career might provide? Are they willing to relocate or to take a cut in pay to establish themselves in a new field? How these questions are answered offers important insight into the clarity and conviction of the client, and how dedicated they are to actually making a change.

What my clients begin to realize is that they are changing not only their careers but their identities as well – the way they interact with the world and way the world interacts with them. They also begin to realize that there are a number of fulfilling things they could do, and that it really does come down to choices, not just one single career. Now comes the realization that this idea of career change is not stagnant or a one-time event. It is fluid and, even more, it is a process of trial and error. As with most things in adult life, patience to allow things to happen is the cornerstone to successful career transitions. It now becomes clear why the earlier information gathering is so important. It reduces the risk of making a decision based on misinformation or lack of information.

As my clients become more skilled at this trial and error part of the process, our time together is coming to an end. They have a clearer vision of their experience and a more sophisticated knowledge base, and I have helped them with perspective and process. We often connect again later around job offers and negotiations strategies once they have settled into a new path.

✳ *In Kevin's case we met twice a month for the first four months. During this time we worked through the Personal Assessment phase. He kept a career journal and I assigned reading and research to expand his knowledge of career opportunities and of the job market. Once that was done, we both felt he could work effectively on his own and we*

*began a once a month schedule. He relocated soon after that and he
contacted me twice by letter with questions. Almost two years to the
day after our first meeting, we met for the last time to discuss the negotiation of his salary and benefits for the accounting firm offer.*✳

Career changers often find the aid of a career counselor
beneficial in this comprehensive planning process. Look for someone who has training, experience and a track record. You'll find
Certified Career Counselors listed in the Yellow Pages, or you
can get the names of those in your area from the National Career
Development Association. Your area colleges and universities
are also another good source for references. My friends and clients continue to insist that this "taking stock" guides them into a
more individualized career plan for themselves and for their future.

B When and How to Use an Employment Agency

Employment agencies should be viewed as one of your marketing tools. Like reading the want-ads, they may not produce the job for you, but you would be foolish to ignore them.

First you should understand that all employment agencies are not the same. Some deal exclusively with temporary workers, others only with permanent placements, and some do a little of everything.

Downsizing has resulted in a burgeoning temporary worker industry, and one that is constantly changing. Part-time professionals totaled more than 4.7 million in 1994. Twenty-eight percent of these were men, and sixty-one percent were employed as engineers, computer scientists, natural scientists, health care providers, teachers, lawyers and the like. Another twenty-six percent were employed in administrative and management related occupations.

Temporary work can have several advantages. It can get you inside companies where the unadvertised jobs are, you can try out jobs and fields before making a commitment, you can learn what "cutting edge" companies are doing in your field. You can acquire and refine practical or technical skills. Temporary work allows you to beef up your resume as you gain valuable work experience.

Like everything else these days, temporary agencies generally specialize in certain types of workers. Some handle only the traditional temporary worker, filling in for sick or vacationing employees or to get rid of a temporary backlog. These jobs are still worth looking at. You'll be getting a paycheck, which will ease the pressure to take just any job. You'll be getting recent experience. You'll be keeping your skills current. You'll get to try different working environments and different jobs. This can be a great place for entry level workers, reentry people and career changers to start, and you'll get plenty of opportunities to practice your interviewing skills.

The downside is the pay probably will not be much. Your stints tend to be brief, so the income will not necessarily be steady. These temporary jobs tend not to be at higher levels of expertise either, and few lead to permanent hires.

Temp-to-hire is a variation on this theme. In this case, if you and the employer are happy with each other after a stated time, you become their employee. These jobs can require more skills and experience. They also give you a chance to try out some options you might not have thought of.

Another form of temporary work is the job shop. These place experience technical people in temporary situations, usually working on a specific project. Project durations vary, from a week or two, to a year or two.

Temporary work for the skilled professional can be attractive, up to $600 a day for top-level managers, although you probably won't get any benefits. However, as the temporary field becomes more permanent, even this is changing.

Employment agencies seek permanent placements. Job levels vary from entry level to highly skilled professionals. These firms are hired by employers, who generally pay them. The jobs they refer you to will be those available at client firms. Although employment agencies are always aware of their applicant pool and keep their ears open for new opportunities, they generally do not go looking for openings outside their client base.

Executive search firms, or "headhunters," seek permanent placement for high level positions especially in upper management and the professional ranks. They also work with highly skilled technical people. Although these firms also work for employer clients, they will go beyond this base for a qualified candidate or someone with unique, hard to find skills.

Your telephone book will probably tell you which agencies do what. You'll want to interview several and you can probably do some initial screening by phone. This is a good way to start, as you'll want to make an appointment with any that fit your needs.

Ask what types of people they specialize in placing. Each is different in their expertise. If they don't want to tell you this, ask how many placements they typically make in your field, advises Gary Kravetz, National Career Choices. Look for an agency with enough counselors to serve their applicants. You'll want someone with enough time to look for a suitable match between you and an employer.

Ask what testing and training programs are available. Some have extensive programs, some virtually none. If programs are available, ask about fees. In fact, ask about fees in general. Some agencies are paid totally by employers, others are not, and there are a variety of fee structures.

You can expect the agency to review your resume and make helpful comments. They'll also tell you where you can realistically find a job and give you some idea of the pay ranges in your field. Many will provide testing for specific job fields.

On your part, be flexible. Be willing to take some risk, advises Cris Wood, Western Staff Services. Be flexible both on salary issues and job descriptions. Be willing to try something out of your norm.

Keep in touch with your agencies, once a week is probably about right. Use as many as fit your needs. Each agency has a different client base, and no one agency knows about all the jobs.

Be responsive when the agency calls and if you accept a temporary assignment, be sure to fulfill your obligation. Otherwise you probably won't get another chance.

Dress for an interview when you visit the agency. You never know. You could be sent right over to a prospective employer.

Index

A

Aburdene, Patricia 96
acceptance/rejection letters 127
accomplishments 40, 43, 145,
    154, 156, 160, 171, 180,
    187
adaptive skills 37
American Association of Retired
    Persons 219
annual report 178
aptitude 19, 39
artistic 18
assertive 172
attitude 2, 8, 34, 59, 67, 168,
    216

B

benefits 101, 134, 136, 138, 189,
    200, 202, 228, 231
body language 182
bonuses 202
budget 219

C

California Employment Develop-
    ment Department 218
California's Job Match 218
career changers 5, 16, 93, 109,
    156, 227
career consumer 95
career counselor 17, 69, 72, 78,
    163, 180, 187, 224

career fairs 98
career objective 145
career planning 6
career trends 100
catalyst 72
challenge 22, 53, 154, 197, 224
chamber of commerce 98
communication skills 41
compatibility 19
competency 19
connections 147
continuing education 202
control 2, 6, 9, 20, 45, 174,
    185, 205, 217, 224
conventional 18
correspondence 127
cover letters 127
creativity 53
current salaries 201

D

downsizing 1, 96, 218

E

Economically Displaced Workers
    Assistance Act 218
education 145, 202
electronic resume 157
emotional salary 49
employment agencies 201
employment statistics 100
enterprising 35
executive recruiters 201
experience 4, 7, 11, 16, 22, 34,
    39, 43, 51, 56, 112, 128,
    144, 147, 150, 154, 164,
    175, 184, 199, 205, 228
experience history 145

Experience Unlimited 218
extroverts 73

F

fear 5, 8, 50, 174, 217
feedback 172, 225
feelers 75
50-30-20 rule 179
field of interest 53
Figler, Howard 36, 49, 147, 216
foreign competition 100
Forty Plus 219
Frankel, Viktor E. 2
functional skills 36

G

global economy 93
Global Paradox, The 96
growth forecasts 100

H

hard skills 37
helping others 52
Hidden Job Market, The 95
high income 52
hobbies 16, 35, 160, 216
Holland, John 18

I

independence 52
industry guides 94
industry specific materials 127
insurance 202

interest 16, 18, 35, 39, 94, 99,
      148, 160, 197, 216, 223
Internet 106, 112, 117, 157

internship 51, 121, 129, 144,
      152, 172, 215, 216, 222
interpersonal relations 53
interview 10, 37, 71, 109, 140,
      145, 154, 163, 171,
      174, 201, 205, 219, 230
introverts 73
intuitives 74
investigative 18
investment 211

J

job description
      101, 136, 150, 178, 201
job fairs 221
job referrals 113
job responsibilities 146, 156
job search 117, 199, 218, 223
job search tools 147
job security 10, 93
Job Training Network 218
judger 76
Jung, C. G. 70

K

Kansas Job Service 218
key words 158

L

leadership 53
leisure 53
library 56, 94, 201, 227
lifestyle 2, 7, 229

M

Megatrends 96
minorities 181

misrepresentation 156
mock interview 180
Motorola 177
Myers-Briggs Type Indicator
    (MBTI) 70

N

Naisbitt, John 96
national issues 94
negotiating 199, 211
new hires 203
non-related jobs 156

O

objection 176
occupational themes 18
organization chart 178

P

parking 202
perceiver 75
periodical indexes 99
personal data base 187
personal management 37
personal time 202
personality style 67
perspective 2, 4, 67, 93, 217
piggy-back 176
portfolio 144
positioning 2, 147
prestige 52
process 7, 38, 71, 140, 179, 215,
    223
procrastination 95
professional affiliations 160
professional organization 103
professional vocabulary 37

Q

query letters 140
questionnaires 141

R

Reader's Guide to Periodical
    Literature 100
realistic 18
reentry 222
references 190
research 4, 59, 93, 130, 179,
    201, 216
research librarians 99
responsibility 7
resume 7, 37, 111, 127, 145,
    187, 219

S

salary 200
sales statistics 100
security 53
self-confidence 11, 20, 181, 184
Self-Directed Search 18
self-esteem 3, 45, 49, 184, 215,
    230
sensors 74
skills bank 35
skills Vocabulary 37
Small Business Administration 98
social 18
soft skills 36
stabilizer 72
state employment center 98
strategic goals 40, 156, 175
Strong Interest Inventory (SII) 17
surveys 100

T

tapes 144
technical skills 37
temporary 220
thinkers 75
trade association 201
trade publications 201
training 35, 51, 111, 145, 152,
        156, 162, 179, 197, 202,
        218, 223
transferable skills 36

U

unemployment 218

V

vacation 202
variety 53
volunteer 40, 121, 144, 147,
        152, 175, 215
volunteer skills 43

W

want ads 93
work experience 16, 42, 71, 128,
        157, 222
writing samples 144

Order Form

Please send me the following publications. I understand that I may return any books for a full refund — for any reason, no questions asked.

UNLIMITED OPTIONS:
☐ **Career Strategies to Last a Lifetime**   **14.97**

AudioTape
☐ **The Professional Self Model - 60 minutes**   **9.97**

Single Topic Pamphlets
☐ **Researching Your Options**   **8.97**
☐ **Interviewing With Confidence**   **6.97**
☐ **Inventorying Your Interests**   **7.97**
☐ **Creating a Convincing Resume**   **7.97**
☐ **Negotiating For a Better Deal**   **4.97**
☐ **Identifying Your Skills**   **5.97**
☐ **Identifying Your Personality Style**   **6.97**
☐ **Correspondence That Sells**   **6.97**
☐ **Determining Your Work Values**   **5.97**

___ Total Publications Ordered   TOTAL _____
Sales Tax (California Residents)   7.75%   _____
Shipping and Handling   1.25
TOTAL AMOUNT   _____
My check in the above amount is enclosed.
Please charge my VISA MC (circle one). _____
Expiration Date _____ Signature: _____

Name: _____
Company: _____
Address: _____
City: _____ State: _____ ZIP: _____
I want to give this powerful information as a gift. Please send the following titles (Your gift will be acknowledged):

_____
To: Name: _____
Company: _____
Address: _____
City: _____ State: ____ ZIP: _____
Mail to: **Prosperity Press**, 1503 Mountain Avenue, Santa Barbara, CA 93101-4725
(Enclose additional sheets if making multiple orders.)

1503 Mountain Avenue
Santa Barbara, CA 93101-4725
(805)963-3028 FAX:(805)963-9272
76656.54@Compuserve.com